## Ley Lines & Earth Energies - The Rediscovery of a Lost Wisdom

### Introduction

Hi, firstly let me say thank you for choosing my book.

It is improbable that anyone will get into this subject by sheer accident; rather, as with Ufology, I sometimes think that earth mysteries research tends to choose *us* – not the other way round; it's as if a universal intelligence, (for want of a better term) is guiding us all in different ways, assigning each person an appropriate life direction – using the most cunning and mysterious operational plan.

My name is Kenneth John Parsons: Privately, I have been a Paranormal and UFO researcher for over 40 years. Publicly, I am the founder/chairman of the British Earth and Aerial Mysteries Society, which was initially set up in 1991, primarily as a non-profit-making studies group, gathering and reporting data pertaining to our particular areas of enquiry.

As well as running B.E.A.M.S. http://www.beamsinvestigations.org/ I have studied the various aspects of Ancient Earth Mysteries, Telluric Energy and Ley Lines for many years, and I am still an active field investigator in the subject.

Earth Mysteries? some might ask - what is that anyway?

Maybe 'mysteries' is not even an accurate description, because as you will learn, for those who have gone before, together with a handful of us still around in this subject, it was never entirely a 'mystery' as such at all.

Sad to say, many will probably not have heard about the topics that I will address in my book; and really, that issue itself demands a big question be tackled; just why is the level of social naivety so high about this subject?

But to those unfamiliar with all of this, don't worry, all will soon be made clear.

For example - although archaeologists tend to roll their eyes at their very mention, and Hollywood makes fun of them... Ley Lines are in fact a reality, something which I will amply demonstrate in Ley Lines & Earth Energies - The Rediscovery of a Lost Wisdom.

Essentially, they are faint natural lines of geological and spiritual/psychic energy that are often marked by various aligned pre-reformation sacred sites plotted out across the Earth.

I will also show how these can point the way to many areas of great interest for all researchers of the Paranormal, UFOs etc.

In this book, you'll learn how to connect such mysterious locations on a map, chart Ley Lines and a great deal more; including how, (and why) under the auspices of the church, most records about our ancient belief in this system have been conscientiously hidden and/or erased.

Really, this is a risky topic to be involved in, because it's so terribly out of fashion; with the subject now being almost invisible on the social media radar, quite a few earth mystery researchers must fear the prospect of having to somehow surmount the massive barrier of incredulity, which is far greater today than ever before.

The situation is such, that I know of quite a few who now prefer to investigate purely on a private basis these days, only sharing their knowledge with those on the same wavelength as it were.

When it comes to trying to inform a largely oblivious public, many specialist researchers like me are likely to see the situation as hardly worthwhile.

I have seen plenty of honest, conscientious investigators who have fallen by the wayside because of this; now unbelieved, ignored and their notebooks, (a lifetime's work in many cases) gathering dust somewhere, destined to be forgotten with them.

Fully aware of the uphill struggle facing me I am carrying on regardless, adopting a take it or leave it attitude; sure, maybe only a relatively few people may ever get to read this and fully appreciate what I have written, but that is better than none at all.

This is one manuscript that isn't going to be left under the bed to be forgotten!

So, I am taking the gamble - it's all or nothing; because, rather than merely giving up and sitting on the wall for fear of ridicule, I am confidently going into battle all guns blazing!

Fully armed with 40 years of experience and an unprecedented mass of evidence, I am determined to reveal as much as I possibly can about this subject; everything I know in fact, hopefully making sense of what others may claim is impossible, unthinkable and incomprehensible.

It is easier said than done to set a book of this kind out in a conventional, regimented order... rationed in the way that most textbooks are designed; so I haven't; instead, the whole thing will be practically one long narrative flow, because everything you find here is intertwining and intimately related... so very hard to divide.

As I am often seeking out fresh evidence of our true past, a project of this nature is, and always will be, an unfinished one; indeed I am constantly updating my knowledge database on Earth Mysteries; but one has to pause and publish at some point, and hopefully you will find the content of what I have gathered so far to date extremely rewarding.

## Conspiracy of Silence

Some might be surprised when I say, that to find the truth these days is extremely difficult - the real uncensored, undiluted truth that is.

But why so? We are supposedly living in *The Information Age* and surely, all worldly facts are now available at our fingertips. Don't kid yourself, because there is much to suggest that the full-blooded type of knowledge we are seeking isn't as freely available as one might assume.

I absolutely promise every reader, that whether it is for constitutional/religious reasons, our past IS constantly being 'airbrushed'... commercially transformed, hyped-up, downplayed/exaggerated or sanitized in some way.

It is beyond mere suspicion, that whenever certain textbooks are first written, or pre-existing texts transcribed, any aspect of our past considered somewhat iniquitous, and which could do with some creative tweaking... will fall prey, whether in one foil swoop or in stages.

Many records are a tissue of omission and evasion; for instance, what might be termed 'social and educational homogenization' is quite common in literature; a cultural memory-stripping about former ways of life, their original meaning and character.

Historical revision is sometimes achieved by deliberate mistranslations of other writing systems; linguistic surgery I call it.

It's always been the same.

As for today, regarding the Internet, you may not find everything you need to know on there either.

My advice is don't believe all of the hype surrounding this medium; it is only as good as the researcher using it; in other words, many times 'Googling' something directly, (the kind of rare info that we are after) will give no results; however, use a 'backdoor' route and your search might be more fruitful.

As can be said about many other things in life, with the Internet, the *obvious* is often the *least* obvious.

Granted, there *are* a small number of interesting pages on the 'net' relating to our line of enquiry, the problem is finding them amongst the dross.

I understand exactly how this system works; unless one knows what to enter into the browser's 'search' box, it can be rather like trawling through a ceaseless stream of nonsense... e.g. propaganda, redundant information, routine text, advertising, fake news and company fanfare.

Also, please note how at the foot of many search pages the following notice is displayed.

*'Some results may have been removed under data protection law in Europe.'*

Try searching for anything too esoteric, (or on a more mundane level, scandals concerning the Royals, politicians, celebrities etc) and that dreaded 'removed' notice is always sat there at the bottom; and this is because now, under the Court of Justice of the European Union, certain users, (usually meaning those with influence) have the right to 'ask' search engines like Google to remove results for queries that include a person's name; that is but one example.

This can mean that those in power, the rich and the famous, now have the right to get their digital footprint totally erased... 'the right to be forgotten' as it is termed; meanwhile back in the real world, the average person has less of a chance to protect themselves in this way and may only get shuffled down the search algorithm if they're lucky... money talks!

This removal of 'names' law has now given the censors free reign; **but I submit that such 'policing of the net goes further. Whenever it comes to certain data that our 'leaders' do not want you to see, (legitimate facts that someone on-high doesn't like, especially anything which might upset social or political issues) then guess what happens? Deleted, disguised, or hidden... simple as; either that, or it was never added to the global computer network in the first place!**

Free speech? What free speech?

**Being slaves to the technology that once promised to free the world, most of us still persist with our 'surfing', even though we can't always find what we want;**

**and that is making some folk miserable... we're fed up with only second-best search results!**

Our over-reliance for instruction from media sources and academic institutions is not healthy; at the end of the day, I reckon that good old-fashioned archival research, via books, museum reading rooms and networking with people, are often more rewarding methods than merely relying on the Internet for fact-morsels.

I am confident that there is a broad conspiracy of silence about a number of issues, and that people are being kept in the dark; **but the greatest secrets of all may concern our misunderstanding about the true dynamics of Planet Earth.**

Anyone just opening the book here randomly, (and let's face it, we all do it) might be scratching their heads as to why orthodox academics/scientists should be tight-lipped about something so seemingly innocuous.

The trouble is for them, we are looking at a welterweight of challenging evidence, not just a few things.

How can this be so - and why? Well, professors of science clearly dislike unexplainable phenomena... anything which cannot be reasoned-away, (excused-away) by orthodox methods; for them, everything must be clear-cut, demonstrable, classified, and pigeonholed.

Let us imagine what would happen then, if someone working at doctoral level, uncovered definitive proof that our universe is far from clockwork and predictable as usually thought? And indeed, I know for a fact that this has happened, as a good number of maverick scientists HAVE attempted to reveal some uncomfortable truths.

What do you think?

Would such a discovery be widely broadcast? or would that news be stifled and the public left blissfully ignorant?

The latter unquestionably.

I myself am not a holder of any degrees, having been too busy hunting for scarce knowledge in the *University of Life*; yet even I can see that the absence of many divergent science philosophies in the public domain smacks of either censorship, suppression and/or intellectual snobbery.

If correct, how then might this problem affect the ordinary man on the street? It would mean that much of what he assumes to be true - is wrong.

Instead of nature's most intimate secrets laying freely available at our fingertips, as one might presume, (through television documentaries, the internet, books and magazines) the public could be in possession of only part-truths; a colouring book version of existence, crammed-full of misleading simplifications.

In our subject, (as with other matters in life) very little is as it appears at first glance; examine many readily available, publicly declared principles or central ideas with excessive scrutiny and invariably one will NOT find clear, crisp boundaries and easy answers.

The solutions to these irregular environments are all about us; they have always been there; it is just that they require different ways of knowing and consideration to the misrepresentations currently being 'sold' to us.

Sure, we are 'free' alright... we are all free to do what we're told – dumbed down and free to think what we are taught to think - free to say what they want us to say, and free to act the way we are expected to behave.

We are all victims of misleading life claims.

In certain ways modern society is in disarray.

Using misinformation, psychological persuasion, and other such *mind games*, we are being subliminally conditioned to never think outside the box of established scientific principle.

Most are convinced that the only people to achieve scientific breakthroughs are those from within academia; whereas in reality, a sizeable number of discoveries are initially made by enthusiastic amateurs, (often by sheer chance) only for those sporting doctorates to come along and lift the glory for their own.

Those 'bright sparks' from the established order teach us that certain things are merely *fanciful* and *impossible*, (such as a planetary/human interconnectedness) even though they were deemed plausible and normal by our distant progenitors.

And vice versa, how we think and behave today would have seemed like fantasy centuries ago.

The popular idea that facts are immutable is a delusion; certainty and logic are always under construction, with each having the distinct tendency to mutate as millennia pass.

From what I have learned, the universe is far more connected than most of our scientific minds would care to confess publicly; even distant stars hundreds of light years away, everything is connected by invisible, barely detectable energy fields and flows.

The easy 'cop out' has always been to fall back on a relaxed view of times-past; by modern standards, the ancients were unenlightened… right? it's as plain and straightforward as that; but fact is, they seem to have been more spiritually intelligent than us.

They knew nothing is 'impossible'; the power of true, untainted 'belief' and thought know no bounds.

Time, that part-artefact of human invention, does tend to play tricks with what is, and what is not bona fide.

The suggestion is, early mythologies might not all be the result of 'primitive fantasy' after all; some were more likely to have been expressions of a special insight on nature and now require a careful re-reading in between the lines.

But really, such withholding of information is nothing new; the truth has always been under suppression.

There are certain literary experts who have put their reputations at risk by arguing that hundreds of historical passages were tampered with and deliberately muddled during translation, and in doing so, much valuable inspiration erased.

'It frequently happened, that the same passage was first corrected by one hand, then corrected back again by someone else to give a quite opposite meaning, according to which dogma was currently the fashion, or a particular school of thought'.

It is supposed however, that the originators might have anticipated future text modifications to an extent and foiled this by writing its most serious messages in cipher.

It is incredible to think, the first treatise ever written on Encryption and Crypt Analysis was discovered in a storage room at Istanbul University... and is 1,200 years old!

The reader will hardly recoil in amazement when I say that here in the UK there has always been a culture of secrecy; we even had our very own College for Cipher Intelligence service back in 1585 or thereabouts! This was founded by Francis Walsingham, who is often referred to as the spiritual father of the modern Secret Service.

Lucky for us, not everything in the way of encrypted text was discovered by the political police.

Here's an example of how we can all look for older texts containing hidden messages.

Magnify certain written data of bygone centuries, (religious works in particular) and one may find 'soul' also being used as a coded substitute for the word 'energy'.

When examining early sacred documents, the first giveaways are any diverse structuring and stress patterns; note the deployment of unusual syntactic placements for emphasis.

**The Past - Our Starting Point**

There are many fallacies written and taught about, often by those from within the highest scholastic circles; and as I say, I am convinced that one of these concerns our planet.

The more I read, the more I realise that there is a message hidden in some old texts... supressed and concealed meanings whose presence can be discovered by anyone. Our distant ancestors knew of this code, and the intelligentsia of today, (any one of the rumoured secret societies that exist for the manipulation of society and world events) now struggles to keep the earliest truth a secret.

My scientific curiosity in all of this was initially piqued by Professor James Ephraim Lovelock, CH CBE FRS (born 26 July 1919) an independent scientist and environmentalist who lives in Dorset.

With a PhD to his credit, he invented the electron capture detector, and using it, became the first to reveal the widespread presence of CFCs in the atmosphere.

While designing scientific instruments for NASA, he developed the Gaia hypothesis, so named after the primordial goddess who personified the Earth in Greek mythology.

Gaia was once a widely held philosophy in which it is postulated that the Earth functions as a self-regulating system... a living, breathing, thinking organism which may be completely unique in the entire universe.

Symbolically, one way of considering Earth as a giant living figure is to think of the soil as its epidermis, or outer skin... rock strata as its frame, air as the lungs, the seas and rivers as its bodily fluids, oil as its blood, all of nature as its brain and Earths' magnetic core the heart.

But there are numerous variations on that theme.

Even now, some Native American religions and various forms of shamanism consider Earth a whole that is greater than the sum of its parts; they see it as a single cell or a single round organism.

Generally, in Eastern and Southern regions, the earth was variously referred to as a 'Goddess' named either 'Astarte', 'Ceres', 'Cybele', ''Demeter', 'Diana' (the Roman Moon Goddess) 'Gaea', (modern Gaia) 'Ishtar', 'Isis', 'Neith' and 'Telluris'.

In the West 'she' tended to be given titles like 'the great corn goddess', 'goddess flora', 'sheila-na-gig' and 'earth hag'.

From this point on though, whenever referring to 'her', said to be the ancestral mother of all life and the very soul of the earth, I will stick to using the name Gaia to avoid confusion.

So, what happens then when us sleepwalkers, (as we might be called) start to hear alarm bells ringing? about how the oceans, air and land are now all under threat? Domesday scenarios describing how future generations will have to face a reign of drought, rising sea levels, disease, horror and confusion?

Then our social engineers kindly reassure us through various TV documentaries, that if ever mankind's survival on planet earth becomes problematical, that continuation of the race will be ensured through Interstellar Colonization.

Why, there must be millions of planetary systems out there likely to contain world's comparable to our own, (they say)... it would be extremely arrogant of us to assume otherwise - so we mustn't go worrying our pretty little heads about the likes of Deforestation, the Greenhouse Effect, Global Warming, Plastic Pollution in our oceans and Over Population.

But here is what they DON'T tell us: It is reckoned that for life to evolve, any planet must have at least three billion years of radiation output from its own sun to generate Earth-type conditions!

Bang goes the cosy dream!

The simple fact is that our home world and solar system are likely to be unique!

Gaia produces her own animating life force imperative for everything, from flora to the highest lifeforms; it is produced by the unification in earth's atmosphere, of Solar Magnetic Forces along with Lunar Rays, combining with favourable Geo Magnetic Energies emanating from within.

How many other planets could boast these attributes?

We must forget this fatuous notion of an exodus to Mars or wherever.

Logic dictates there is probably only one earth - and if we damage her, our planet has a nasty way of kicking back.

At this point, I expect swift opposition by many examiners to any such proposal; enough is enough; I can't read anymore! it's a natural tendency I know, but exactly what triggers this automatic reflex action of denial in us? The answer, I am sure, is years of social programming... brainwashing us into believing that our earth is simply a lump of rock spinning in space; and with such bog-standard education filling our heads, this is what causes many people to reject posits contradicting the scientific establishment.

Most scholars understand that their livelihoods are on the line, should they ever deviate too far away from the traditional textbooks; so, they continue to lecture their university indoctrinations copycat-fashion, reluctant to ever query them.

Very few of a maverick calibre have been brave enough to expose the veil of censorship that they are forced to work under, all for their fear of becoming blacklisted, academic outcasts or being labelled 'lunatic fringe'... with such twisted logic making good financial sense to them; and when someone has dared to blow the whistle on the whole charade, it has often been following their resignation or dismissal, with them revealing what they know through relatively underground methods such as 'vanity', (private) publishing or more adventurously, through the small lecture circuit.

So, the Gaia theory - hated by scientists, loved by the public. This is a paradox with a deep history, and those who are wide awake to this discussion may now want to read further.

Using maps, dowsing, some psychic intuition and my self-taught ability to accurately 'read' the landscape, along with any data gleaned from book and document study, (which involved searches for long-forgotten social customs, legends, folklore etc) together with my partner Hilary, we regularly go on pilgrimages to hunt for traces of small ancient holy places; these include healing wells/springs, Pagan shrines, (by the way, 'Pagan' is simply a word which originally meant 'countryman') and the remnants of hidden landscape effigies, all of which are usually key marker points on earth energy pathways.

On our journeys, we have hit upon just a handful of the larger sites which still retain much of their sacredness; fairly-free from too much commercialization, these places are best described as natural geo-psychic 'power points'. No coincidence either that all these favoured spots exist in tracts of country which possess a long mystical/historical pedigree, stretching back thousands of years, including folk memories of magic ritual.

Despite having their secrets firmly locked in the land, we have witnessed people spending hours at these centres, with some sitting and meditating come rain or come shine, many subconsciously attempting to connect back into nature's rhythm.

Some of these places will be listed on forthcoming pages.

Though fact and myth do have the knack of becoming mixed together over time, it should always be considered that in every tablespoon full of myth, there exists a teaspoon full of truth.

I begin with Avebury, Wiltshire.

When it comes to souvenir shop literature about Avebury, much of this tends to be coffee table eye-candy; packed from cover-to-cover with glossy pictures, demure essays about skeletal remains and sketched reconstructions of men working with flints, bone tools etc; fine, if that is your bag, but hardly convincing for me.

I suspect that most books for sale at these places are purposely selected to please day-tripper-types and designed so as not to tread on any toes; with political correctness always in mind, the compilers of these works assume that people do not want to read about certain speculations, however well-founded.

Skilful opinion is what these publications lack... such as regarding the ceremonies that were practised at these and other stone enclosures; how primal man seems to have had a matriarchal bond with the Earth; and how his special sites were more than likely an open-air equivalent of our grandiose cathedrals, constructed as gateways to communicate with the earth and celestial gods.

And hard fact... such as how controlled experiments conducted by independent teams of geo-specialists have uncovered a sonorous component to certain megalithic installations; in other words, some ancient sites possess strange acoustic properties! They have actually pinpointed occasional emissions of ultrasonic frequencies coming from these places!

These were mainly measured at 3khz.

We are rarely asked to consider just why their enduring structures were so well built; which might have been because they were designed as legacies, each containing a symbolic language, intended to be passed on through successive generations?

Many of the old traditions are vestiges of a great reality.

None of this data is as radical as it may first come across, yet such things have rarely played a part in the vocabulary of the average archaeologist/historian; and here we see the prime cause why these buildings have often been the target of constant architectural suspicion and controversy through the epochs.

For all intents and purposes, guidebook 'glossies' are aimed at the pre-programmed thinker and rarely contain philosophy or anything outside of the norm.

As per usual, it is the things we are not normally told, (or sold) which ultimately turn out to be the most essential.

Sharp-eyed researcher David Icke, author of *The Biggest Secret*, is never afraid to speak his mind; although his exposes might not appeal to every taste, pages 63-7 are a must-read for any serious investigator of earth mysteries.

Mr Icke busily goes to work grappling with ancient accounts about Avebury's esoteric background.

This is just a very small but significant taster of *TBS*, a section which is devoted to Avebury, its builders and its numerous Ley Lines, geodetic lines, (same thing... an energy path between two points on the earth's surface) or 'meridians' as David also terms them... invisible rays not marked on any tourist itinerary maps.

'Brian Desborough, my scientist friend from California, told me that there is a point on one of the earth grids, the Hartmann Grid as it is called, where twelve of these force lines meet and go down into the earth.'

Where was that? I asked: 'a place called Avebury in (Wiltshire) England' he said.

'The very place that the advanced Phoenician-Sumerians chose to build their stone circles at least five thousand years ago, along with a series of surrounding sites, including Silbury Hill.' End quote.

To be honest, confirming the accuracy of Mr Desborough's claims would be unworkable for me or anybody else, but I must say that they do have a ring of truth about them.

And there are other calculations about this place, made by some noteworthy people, which reveal an accuracy that is almost beyond belief.

Regarding the siting of Avebury's stone complex itself, Robert LaMont – Mich. DHP. DCH. who is an authority on Avebury, has advised us about two incredible links between the sarsen sanctuary there and the Great Pyramid, Giza, Egypt.

He has pointed out that: Avebury's main stones have a cartographical latitude of precisely 51.51 degrees and the slope of the Great Pyramid measures the same... 51.51 degrees!

On their own, these figures might be considered just plain lucky, but combined with the next astonishing set of statistics, the suggestion is that most prehistoric sacred sites around the world share a familiar ancestry.

**Celestial Reflections in Rainfall Mirrors**

Nearby Silbury Hill possesses a slope angle of exactly 30 degrees, and surprise, surprise, the latitude of the Giza Plateau site is the same - 30 degrees!

**Neolithic Silbury Hill, surrounded by flood water, near Avebury, Wiltshire, UK**

This masterpiece of landscape architectural engineering which towers over Avebury, is at least 4.400 years old.

Officially recognised as the largest artificial prehistoric mound in Europe, Silbury stands some 40 metres, (130 feet) tall and is estimated to have taken 18 million man-hours to construct.

What would have originally been a broad, deep ditch around the hill has become relatively shallow now due to it being naturally filled with centuries of plant silt; but even so, when it floods during wet spells 'the hill looks like it's floating on its own sea'.

This could so easily have been some form of temple with the water reflecting the night sky... in other words, a celestial mirror for Neolithic Sky Watchers!

According to those who manage Silbury Hill and Avebury, the true purpose and significance of these mystical spots remain unknown; but despite the English-Heritage-endorsed rejection of 'fringe' ideas, there are some unambiguous facts and figures that cannot be dismissed; and for me, such accuracy in the design of Avebury and Silbury Hill does suggest the possibility of Phoenician-Sumerian involvement - and that Brian Desborough's assessment was likely to be correct.

Sadly, by 1837, the majority of Neolithic standing stones at Avebury had gone, having been either buried by pious locals in the 14th century or smashed up for building materials in the 17th and 18th; but investors who backed a scheme to recycle the stone were bankrupted when the houses they built proved to be unsaleable and also prone to burning down.

However, during the 1930s archaeologist Alexander Keiller unearthed and re-erected many of the megaliths there - and helpfully marked those permanently lost with concrete posts.

We now see that relying on the censored confines of archaeological textbooks and religious teaching is pointless; much of what we assume to be certainty is inaccurate and distorted.

Archaeological finds and folk memory/myths, (many of which are based on actual facts, practices and customs) suggest, that since the earliest existence of mankind we have found comfort from material objects; whether that was simply an interestingly-shaped rock that primeval man picked up in a field, or otherwise something he created by hand such as a giant earthen sculpture!

Ambitiously, using deer-antler picks and shoulder-blade shovels, teams of workers would sometimes fashion oversize earth and chalk carvings, of god-men or other types of earth-mother effigies and delineate them by durable cobbled or otherwise paved trackways through which the divine representation's power was encouraged to be present.

The Long Man of Wilmington, Sussex; mysterious guardian of the South Downs who has baffled archaeologists and historians for hundreds of years.

With early mankind though, I suspect that their satisfaction with the simple things in life didn't result from them not having the choice for this to be any other way; no, my researches show me that there was something far deeper going on with our ancestor's thankfulness and admiration of nature.

They instinctively bonded with nature, on which they relied upon heavily for their survival both physically and spiritually; they possessed an almost child-like reverence for the living powers of creation.

They let the planet be their teacher and automatically opened their minds to the secrets of nature and natural law.

Example, I have learned that in the early Ethiopian cultures, if someone wanted to extract some clay from the ground to make a pot, that person would either verbally or mentally seek/request permission of the primordial earth mother goddess to do so.

Guidance would come through in the form of 'signs', which was most likely the interpretation of natural phenomena. Similarly, if someone wanted to fell a tree in order to create something, permission would always be earnestly and humbly sought from the earth out of sheer respect and reverence; for it was told that to ignore this would spell disaster, such was the level of people's superstition in those days.

The oldest belief systems were goddess and woman centred.

This was a universal concept, a widely shared set of beliefs amounting to the earliest form of religion.

Up until about 2000 years ago, societies in Britain were basically peaceful and honoured women; until that is, our country was changed by the arrival of the Romans whose patriarchal culture saw men holding primary power and predominate in roles in religion and political leadership.

Throughout the Roman occupation of Britain, the strong overhauling the weak was a reoccurring theme; yet our cultural transformation from Paganism to Christianity wasn't an overnight conversion by any means; it was gradual... and steadily, out went the old 'primitive notions'; then under Roman rule, women began to be portrayed as subordinate.

It is clear to see that things went terribly wrong with society back then; and to say that religion was to blame would be no exaggeration. Here is one current, official statistic of precisely what religion has done to humanity over the millennia; the most famous estimate is there have been 56 million human deaths due to religious warring; but even a more critical conservative examination would STILL put Christianity's death toll at a *mere* 9.064 to 28.734 million!

Having blindly accepted the 'barbaric' and 'faithless' tags that our educators have put on Paganism, most would say *never in a million years* would they entertain anything to do with this way of life; yet, like it or not, our ancestors might have been onto something!

Yet, for a lot of people, it would be unthinkable to 'go back' and begin reviving dead legends; performing old, quaint or picturesque practises, such as the formulaic use of evocation symbols, because for one thing, our conscious knowledge of the meaning of those rites is largely lost thanks to state suppression.

And we are not only discussing the UK here, it has been a largely worldwide effort; just check out this paper headline from Colorado, U.S., dated September 25, 2014.

*Students and educators in Jefferson County, Colorado, are pushing back against their school board's proposal to whitewash U.S. history: "The Danger of Censoring Our History" is how they describe their school's policy of banning certain books.*

Although the aforementioned is more to do with the identification and weeding out of materials that encourage or condone civil disorder, social strife or disregard of the law...

https://www.boarddocs.com/co/jeffco/Board.nsf/files/9NYRPF6DED70/$file/JW%20PROPOSAL%20Board%20Committee%20for%20Curriculum%20Review.pdf

...it is clear, that selective bits have been, and are still are being, excised from the carcass of history... a fact being acknowledged by an increasing number of educators and students.

Using any method at their disposal - our censors will seize the opportunity.

**Beware of Those Etymological (His) Story Books**

Take popular place name dictionaries for instance.

In order to get as close to the truth as possible, I have been forced to track down some pretty obscure commentaries about our pre-Christian past; additionally, my inquiries have been aided by studying philology, (the branch of knowledge that deals with the structure and historical development of words) along with comparative linguistics; as a result, I can now assuredly issue a warning to anyone relying purely on popular dictionaries of English place-names and similar academic reference sources; take these 'probably refers to' (this and that) *OE* name guessing exercises with a massive pinch of salt!

Problem is that, half of the time scholastic graduates contracted to create the Etymological data books/internet pages are working on assumption.

Yes, yes, we know that Anglo-Saxon place names are to be found everywhere. Towns ending with the suffix -**ton** (the OE for 'farmstead'), or -**ham** ('homestead'), or -ley ('wood'), or containing an -**ing** (OE for 'the people of' or 'belonging to', hence the Vikings may be 'the people of the fjord'), but these don't tell us what we truth seekers REALLY want to know.

At best, it must be considered that mainstream 'English' of the early time periods, (the lack of education meaning worse pronunciation of names thereof) geographic isolation, and many 'sub-dialect/languages', would mean that certain indigenous names of unowned public locations and spaces have, in all likelihood, been lost, subsequently 'misunderstood' or are being overlooked altogether; and perhaps deliberately so.

The trouble I find, it is the latter century titles fabricated for land privatization by nobility, (added simply to suit the wealthy landlords of that time) which were/are mostly employed by Etymologists in their examinations.

The first explanation for this is likely to be researchers operating on an inadequate budget, (and/or laziness?); the second explanation is much uglier; it may be for a very dark reason that some essayists of old were instructed to patch over any evidence holes in our history chapters using the *Pollyfiller* of deceit.

And contemporary writers copy parrot-like.

Yet, despite the labours of those I suspect who have/are (either deliberately or inadvertently) distorted/distorting our past, (conceivably in order to influence and further an agenda) miraculously, some important clues DO still exist.

There are even country/nation names where a remnant of reference to Pagan deity faith still survive; for example, look for appellations with the 'Ma' syllable in their title.

I won't spoon-feed the reader too much at this point, because there are enough stubborn identifiers around to keep them busy - as will soon become clear; here's one quick specimen though, (and remember, the 'Ma' syllable may be placed anywhere in a word, either at the opening, middle or end)... A '**MA**' ZON: The Amazons were known as warriors who worshiped the Moon and the goddess of the green petticoat.

And please note, even where 'Ma' is not the prime syllable, chances are there will be districts within any given country that will have their 'Ma' giveaways.

Take Sudan for instance… no direct 'Ma' clue there in that name - but wait, Sudan contains specific regions that DO begin with 'Ma'; including **Ma**jeigha, **Ma**ridi and **Ma**rawi to quote but a handful.

I chose Sudan as a case in point, after remembering having watched an old documentary called 'Vanishing World', which again made me realise just how prevalent planet worship still is in places, even among some modern natives.

In the programme a Sudanese guide could be heard excitedly pointing out regions of his sacred territory to the film crew, using these very words; **'this low-lying swamp is our mother's groin; and this dry upland is her head'.**

**Make no mistake, look up the name roots of these places on the net and quite often, the truth about their polytheistic, (and often female deity-based) origins will have been carefully skirted around; although sometimes the truth is unavoidable, no matter how good the modern specialists are at re-writing facts.**

Contrary to my concerns expressed so far, oddly, I have noticed that the greatest number of 'Ma' words are what I would call of a positive nature; how strange is that? And yet the total of what might be considered as derogative 'Ma' terms is miniscule in comparison; it's as if a trick was missed! Here's an off-putting one though to illustrate what I'm talking about; it is said that the word **'Mayhem'** is an open condemnation about the reported confusion witnessed during public 'May Holy Days' or coming of Spring celebrations!

Now for a positive: **Pacha<u>mama</u>** is the highest divinity of the Aymara and Quechua peoples, the protector goddess of all material things.

High atop the Andes, indigenous Bolivians hold a traditional sacrifice to honour Pachamama, the goddess of the earth and fertility, Wednesday, the Day of Mother Earth.

Believers rise at dawn to give respect and burn their offerings to ask Mother Earth for her blessings. In Bolivia's traditionally agricultural society, farmers offer up vegetables, fruits, and animals from their farms, believing that Pachamama will bless them with good crops and wealth. The celebration is held across the North of Argentina and Chile through Peru and Bolivia.

See how many good, proven examples you can come up with!

This type of search should be an easy one for starters, as much of these thinly veiled mentions are there 'buried' in plain sight, (another instance of the obvious being the least obvious) right under your very nose as it were; the truth has been staring you in the face for years. Some of these ideas may prove to be fruitful, while others less so; really, unearthing the best nuggets of information all comes down to open-mindedness, inquisitiveness, and dogged determination on the part of the researcher.

**Later, we will see how many general words have been cleverly structured, (or camouflaged) to discretely commemorate our Pagan past.**

There will be those looking in who will insist that all of this is just too easy to be true.

It is a common trap to fall into... insisting that something so obvious could not possibly have alluded the attention of modern classical scholars; but that's just the paradox, I don't think it has.

I am not alone in such thinking, plenty of other specialists have also discovered the same poorly papered-over cracks in records of our past.

I know this to be certain, because there are quite a few cases where some brave lecturer chose to speak out publicly on the matter, only to be silenced by character assassination, and/or dismissed as a crank with an over-active imagination.

The professional dissenter will always make excuses for the structuring of these words and will likely try accusing me of taking things out of context or advancing obsolete and obtuse nonsense to back my claims.

They may conveniently overlook any academic question marks surrounding the birthplace and usage of 'Ma', particularly those working with etymology as a profession; conveniently overlooking how, when one attempts to trace the stem or intent behind this syllable in reference works, it is so often labelled by the compiler as being 'of unknown origin', 'ambiguous origin' or some-such description to the same effect.

The impression I am getting after studying so much of this stuff, is one of an antique dialect now almost covered by orthographical changes and embellishments.

Seldom are it's battered remains obvious, with only some primary accenting, phonetic features, folklore and customs left for the sharp-eyed to work with; fragments regarding Earth Mother/Earth Energy dedications which need some loving restoration using sound-right reasoning.

How we got to this sorry state-of-affairs is easy to work out with a bit of back engineering.

It is a sad fact of human nature, but because the 'wisemen', (shamanic priests and other knowledge holders) were most likely viewed as a severe threat to Catholic missionary work here in Britain, and so a great deal of negative proPAGANda was circulated by the church attacking Wiccans and their lifestyles.

That created a gross misconception regarding Paganism in general; and this continues to be firmly imbedded within the public psyche of today.

Concerning Freemasonry and their Pledge of Fidelity, The Third Degree reads: *'the secrets of nature and the principles of intellectual truth were then unveiled to your view.*

*To your mind, thus modelled by virtue, science and nature present one great and useful lesson more.*

***She*** *prepares you, by contemplation, for the closing hour of existence, and when, by means of contemplation,* ***she*** *has conducted you through the intricate windings of this mortal life,* ***she*** *finally instructs you to die.'* End quote.

Note the consistent references to a female deity? (one could hardly miss them!)

From what I have learnt, the brethren of this founding order became guardians of an ancient insight; the very same knowledge that the Church of Rome were attempting to stamp out in society all over.

In the Gnostic texts, ('Gnostic' is Greek for knowledge) it specifies; 'there are three powers: The high God, who is most powerful; Elohim, the male God and co-creator with his female partner... and EDEM/Eden, **Mother Supernal of The Earth**, (the Garden of Edem) who is clothed with the Sun and Moon at her feet'.

Now isn't that intriguing? And notice how we don't normally get to hear about this kind of thing? Generally, all we are told about the early times is either in the form of Disneyfied pap or unreadable Ph.D. -style monographs... leaving folk verging on the border of mental malnutrition; and those who are starved of the truth often seek solace through escapism.

It's an everyday scene, people relaxing in front of the *box* and enthusiastically being *told what to do by the 'telly'*; gorging themselves on an electronic illusion, watching game shows and soap operas; meanwhile, others busily feed their brains with Harry Potter and Arthurian romances; maybe even adorning their homes with colourful resin-cast ornaments of dragons, Merlinesque wizards, princesses and warriors.

It's almost as if the people of today subconsciously know they are being lied to, about how we used to live so long ago and are attempting to fill this information void with fantasy.

These quick fix solutions long term may only further serve to foster ignorance about our true past.

Much remains deftly hidden, and judging by our exhaustive enquiries, the level of public unawareness concerning true Paganism is quite astounding.

Our perception about the Green Man belief is but a single facet of this general unfamiliarity.

Green Man is an image which is found most tellingly in early Churches, carved in stone or wood as a slightly humorous face, often depicted with foliage sprouting from his mouth, nose, eyes, ears or as hair.

Such foliate heads are said to represent tree worship and fertility; this type of iconography is thought by some to be a remembrance of a long-forgotten way of life.

If one thousand people were polled and asked if they knew anything about this character, one of the most ancient fertility gods, the archetype of our oneness with the earth... how many would even have a clue? beyond that is, a memory of seeing such faces as ornaments for sale at garden centres?

A few might guess at 'oh, it's a Pagan image, from the time of bloody ritual' – 'it's just superstitious nonsense' - 'where humans were sacrificed, then decapitated and their heads paraded around on poles as offerings to the tribal gods'.

Not quite, now let us pull back and try to make sense of this.

In reality... The Green Man image is pre-Christian certainly, but most of the prejudices that we harbour about practices from that period are likely to have been exaggerated thanks to religious misinformation.

Images of the bearded man, (as seen here in the 16th/17th century jug shown above) were once common decorations on utilitarian wares; yet, even this was originally based on the early Green Man of western European mythology, but later attributed to Cardinal Bellarmine, who was much maligned in England at a time of religious upheaval.

Despite being found in scattered pockets across Europe, regions of Asia and Africa, few lands have more to show in the way of Green Man tradition than Great Britain.

Our controllers tell us how the Dark Ages were unenlightened times; one could expect to encounter brigands at every thicket and a hanged man on every branch'; stories of plagues, disease, filth, vermin, jugglers and minstrels complete the cliché.

Of course, some of that is most definitely true, but to believe this is practically all there was in the lives of our Pagan ancestors would be naïve to say the least.

The truth now laid bare, tells us that, apart from town life and its mundania, an intriguing world existed.

There was another side to those days of poverty, chronic infectious diseases, and similar hardships, but few are in any great hurry to go against the grain and report on the matter.

From everything taught, I have found that most agrarian communities, (rustic folk) of this period adopted a holistic approach to life.

Living nature was seen in terms of interacting wholes, (as of living organisms) instead of the sum of its parts.

The higher proportion who abided by this venerable code, were basically all farmers or 'Land Husbands', those dedicated to serving Gaia.

Land husbandry dated from the Neolithic revolution when animals were first domesticated, around 13,000 BC onwards.

The remainder was made up of more priestly types - descendants from the archaic caste; those whose teachings were passed down orally from grand master to student.

These were societies' shaman, seers and healers, the scientists, and doctors of their day.

Although the information that we are seeking often hails from many hundreds of years ago, sometimes, the more relatively recent, Victorian and Edwardian analects, (in particular, material discovered in the Agricultural Museum archives of Reading, Berkshire) proved just as fruitful to this enquiry.

Nestling near some of the more predictable farming books in the Museum collection, I came across a very interesting Edwardian journal; in one section of this it detailed *how those who sought to 'purify' society of its heathenish ways, completely outlawed all forms of Druid and Wiccan land ceremony.*

Steadily, those who wouldn't come around to the prescribed church ideology, were forced into conducting their affairs away from prying eyes.

All of this might seem an eternity from the McDonald's disposable culture we are living in presently, but back then, at a time of distress and limited life expectancy, faith in the earth goddess and her associates, great care and fertilization of the terrain, (with land husband's being practically wedded to the earth) was the norm; this would have acted as a kind of insurance policy... with mock sacrifices and votive offerings presented to the deities in return for healthy crops/livestock, and the protection of loved ones.

Where do you think that the concept came from for farmers to stand a crude shape of a man fashioned from sticks and old clothes out in their fields, viz. – the scarecrow?

In many instances, prior to Britain's 'industrial revolution', (before most Gaia sentiments had been abandoned) the scarecrow you know of these days would have originally been a large willow man, (up to 12 metres tall) – yes, a carefully-woven Wicker Man - an offering to the supernatural divinities.

Downgraded/Degraded: From Wicker Man Gaia offering – to rag-wearing Scarecrow

The' Corn Dolly', (or 'Kern Baby') and even the 'Wicker Cross', which are diluted recalls of early environmental contributions... (customs originally dating back to a period before monarchical reign, land and fiscal feudalism, taxation, the church and politics reared their ugly heads) also played a part.

These distinct representations based their trust on the confidence that our biosphere is alive... a prehistoric paradigm which some now are beginning to recognize as scientific fact.

Respected South-African born writer Dr Lyall Watson, acknowledges how the Pagan images of Gaia and those who were thought to help her, go way beyond being symbols of basic procreation; they could easily represent the Hyperdimensional Forces of what he calls 'Supernature'.

Another notable author Colin Wilson, says 'the earth itself is a living body, and its surface is permeated with magnetic forces that are influenced, like the tides, by heavenly bodies, particularly the Moon.'

These forces are not purely magnetic or electrical – they can interact with the human mind'. End quote.

## Moon Madness?

Every so often we are instructed by our scientific maestros that earths' companion the Moon is magnetically weak, and, (apart from controlling the tides) it can exert no influence over our planet – or us.

Never mind the fact that our ancestors swore by Lunar Planting, (they must have all been loonies – LUNes... right?) Planting would have taken place just before a new moon because traditionally, seed sown when the moon is waning is not known to thrive; and in a similar vein, harvesting and storing of crop used to be conducted during the full moon. [or the 'night-sun']

Whenever authorities on the topic get a chance to sneak this old chestnut into their narrative, this is what they tell us; and frighteningly we hang on to every word of our instructors... the Moon doesn't really matter in the great scheme of things.

Either our 'experts' haven't got the brains they were born with or they are lying to us, that is all I can say.

The influence of the Lunar Rhythms over larger botanical and animal groups has always been known about... as this old farmers' rhyme suggests:

'Sow beans when the moon is round, they'll pod down to the ground.'

A sound knowledge of the Moon Calendar used to be of the utmost importance to those involved in agriculture for achieving good yields.

In the early part of the 20th century, numerous trials proved beyond doubt, that the seeds of certain plants, (farmed cereals, leaks, and yarrow in particular) thrived and yielded a large harvest when planted two days prior to a full moon.

Naturally, some of today's hi-tech farmers would probably laugh at the very mention of Moon-related phenomena; but animal husbandry workers the world-over have long been aware how our Moon regulated the behaviour of livestock; mating patterns alter during certain lunar phases; there are more births, animal eating habits changes and egg laying can increase markedly.

The Moon affects humans equally.

Idioms such as 'moon madness', 'bark at the moon' and 'cry for the moon' are all self-explanatory.

Would the average person even know that our Moon plays an integral role in the beliefs of Islam?

First called DINA AL ISLAM, ('Dina' being the Earth and Lunar Goddess, known in other cultures as 'Diana') the Islamic calendar still continues to be purely lunar in its marking of time, with a year ten days shorter than the 'tropical' year.

This ancient belief is also reflected in the décor of mosques and other areas of the Islamic faith, where Crescent Moon symbolism is repeatedly displayed.

 And if there is nothing to this, (as some are sure to suggest) then why has this practice lasted so long, with millions of followers?

There must be something very special about this belief; I've even found suggestions that man formerly recognised the Moon as being of equal importance to the solar body!

Might it even be the case that we didn't always sleep by night and work by day? instead, ancient man may have been a creature of the night during Spring and Summer months in particular, practicing Lunar gardening/harvesting as well as his associated customs and rituals along the Ley Lines.

And… what is the Black Stone of Mecca?

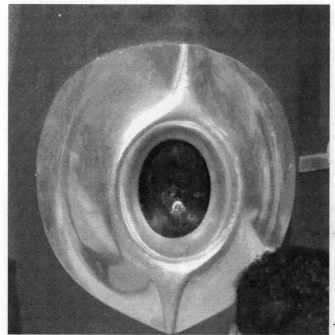 The Black Stone of Mecca or Kaaba Stone is a Muslim holy relic, which according to Islamic tradition dates back to the time of Abraham, (Ibrahim) and his son Ishmael, (Ismail). It is located inside the Kaaba, an ancient sacred building to which the Muslims pray in the center of the Grand Mosque in Mecca, Saudi Arabia.

The 'Stone' comprises of two large, dark rock fragments, polished smooth over time by the hands of millions of pilgrims and is protected by a silver frame nailed to the stones in the side of the Kaaba.

Many have described the Kaaba stone as a meteorite.

I don't know about many of you, but I certainly get the feeling of being cheated educationally; I certainly wasn't taught about things like this at state school.

Sure, they made me learn about The Battle of Hastings in 1066 and algebra… blah, blah, blah, but who needs useless info like that in real life?

I wonder, just how many people like me have been, (and still are being) deliberately misled, misinformed or simply not briefed at all on the most important elements about our heritage.

The cult of Earth Mother is the oldest and most popular belief system.

During the Pagan ages there was such a placental attachment to Gaia that agricultural farmers the world over, often betrothed themselves to 'her', quite literally, and in a very physical way!

Up until a few decades ago, in some Nubian regions this same vogue, (as wild as it may sound) was still prevalent.

Here is one citation that sums things up.

Farmers of the Akamba tribe, East Africa, were once so vehement about Gaia that they would drill small vertical holes into farmland, where initiates took it in turns to copulate with and fertilise what they call the 'Earth Wife'. (Ouch!)

The Kamba or Akamba people are a Bantu ethnic group - or tribe, who live in the semi-arid formerly Eastern Province of Kenya stretching east from Nairobi to Tsavo and north up to Embu, Kenya. This land is called Ukambani which constitutes of Makueni County, Kitui County and Machakos County.

As for British and European land husbands, they were known to *masturbate over the winter seeds of wheat and rye, and the freshly tilled soil, (a practise known as *semen yemale*); same went for their Lenten seeds, oats, barley, vetches, peas and beans, (a routine known as *semen quadragesmale*).

That kind of thing was customary right up until about the 15th century. (*information obtained courtesy of 'English Villagers of the Thirteenth Century' by George Casper Homans' and published by Harvard University Press, 1942).

It makes one think.

Who could deny how much of the Bible is given over to practical wisdom about agriculture? now compare what is going on in the previous scene to a passage from Genesis 38: v. 8&9…'and he spilled his seed on the ground'.

Then we have the psychosexual symbolism involved throughout old-style farming… full-stop!

Reflect on the phallic imagery of 'heavy horses' dragging ploughshares, harrows and other ground-impregnating irons; and how between them they create the thoroughly feminine 'furrow'.

As John Alden Mason Ph. D and former curator of the American Museum of Natural History says:

'She', (earth) was the one most supplicated by the common farmer.'

In Irish Folk Ways by E. Estyne Evans 1957, (page 188 Turf and Slane) it is explained how in northern Ulster, the thin top layer of the mountain bogs used to be removed 'with a variant of the breast-plough, known as a flachter or flaying spade, one of the tools which this region shares with western Scotland. The term **breast-plough** is a euphemism, for it is really a **groin-plough**, pushed forward by thrusts of the thighs and **groin**. '

**The breast-plough**

A very rare old piece of farming history. It is sometimes called a 'breast plough' but its use was for 'paring' or slicing the turf or stubble prior to ploughing. The implement would be pushed along with the worker well-padded in the lower body area! With a deft twist the turf would be turned over to be dried and recycled as fuel or compost.

*God Speed the Plough* was once a popular old catchphrase! How many readers are aware that in Medieval times, Ploughs or 'Plows' themselves were sometimes blessed in the church and dragged through the streets in celebration?

One adjudicator of ancient matters described our former traditions succinctly when writing:

*'The earth under which men are buried is the Mother of the dead. The acceptance of such an explanation would have an important effect on the construction of burial places.*

*The object of the tomb builder, (Neolithic) would have been to make the tomb as much like the body of Mother as he was able.'*

*'The same idea seems to have been carried out in the internal arrangements of the passage grave, with the burial chamber and passage representing the uterus and vagina'*. T. Cyriax. Archaeological Journal, 1921, vol. 28, pp205 -15.

He saw the undulating countryside as Earth Mothers' fertile belly, and below ground lay her uterus from which all nature emerged.

Caves held a vaginal analogue for him, and upon death he would have wished to be returned to the giant sacred womb; subterranea was the choice place of entombment for expected Rebirth, Reincarnation or Resurrection!

For reinforcement of the aforesaid, one should examine similarities between the word's 'Womb' and 'Tomb', and the way that Neolithic burial often involved corpses being interred in the foetal position.

The Green Man was a very important player in the whole Pagan outlook.

The ageless blade of verdant is a classical piece of anthropomorphism... a deity attributed with the capability of manifesting in the shape of a mystical entity.

GM is further identified with the adventurous English hero Robin Hood.

Legend tells of how Robin Hood or 'Wood', (as it is sometimes given) robbed the rich and gave to the poor from his encampment in Sherwood Forest, Nottinghamshire.

Medieval ballads give Robins' first companions as Will Scarlet and George-A-Green, then later came Maid Marian and Friar Tuck.

Robin reputedly met his end after a nun stabbed him to death near Kirklees Priory, Halifax in 1247.

I am convinced that the entire tale is allegorical… a vehicle used to symbolise a deeper spiritual or moral meaning.

Firstly, the name of Robin's partner Maid Marian catches my eye.

'Marian' literally means 'of or pertaining to the Virgin Mary'; from L. L 'Maria'. 'Mary'.

Then there is the special importance placed on Robin's green apparel; and what about the curious name of his side-kick George-A-Green? As well as the way the hero is eventually killed by a Catholic sister.

But my greatest misgiving that Robin Hood ever existed as a person, is raised by similar tales of a green-suited outlaw which had subsisted in Anglo Saxon, hobgoblin mythology long before Norman rule began!

As philosophies propounded by Plato and Pythagoras indicate, Green Man is a leftover from a religion based on anima telluris, (Latin for 'Animated Earth')… a conviction where our planet was thought of as one entire Living Being, kept alive by specially assigned, supernatural, biological and ecological forces, which in turn had to be spiritually nourished by man.

According to Plato in the *Timaeus*, our universe is 'one whole of wholes' and 'a single living creature that contains all living creatures within it.' And it was first in the *Timaeus* that Plato described the 'World Soul', (which is literally the soul of the cosmos) as 'the intelligent and harmonious principle of proportion or relatedness that exists at the heart of the cosmic pattern and allows the living world to unfold in the best possible way.'

This primeval mindset dictated that everything, both animate and inanimate, possessed exceptional virtues, and each was part of the great Earth Goddess.

Gaia's representative was the fertility god Green Man.

He was known by a variety of titles through the ages, with names like 'oak king', 'holly king', 'jack', 'green jack', Robin Goodfellow', 'John Barleycorn', 'Herne The Hunter', 'Pan' and 'wild man of the woods'.

His leafy image personified many things including:

- The forces of nature
- Man's collective responsibilities as caretakers of the environment

and

- Irrepressible life, virility, fruitfulness, and the propagation of our species.

In Latin, (the earliest language of the church) the masculine vitality within nature was often referred to as the 'animus'.

'She', (Gaia) on the other hand, was seen as the 'anima', the feminine mother, lady of sagacity, mystery and magic.

Make no mistake, the icons of Green Man and the nature goddess are archetypal and were once as globally popular as the Christian cross is today.

In fact, his image has never truly died away; the Green Man motif even enjoyed a revitalisation in the 19th century, becoming a popular face carved on furniture and even artistry on tavern/public house signage during a trend known as Gothic Revival.

The Green Man is a metaphor – meaning something else, something far deeper in our psyche... a genetically inherited, subconscious remembrance of a former belief system.

Amongst others, the essence of these classical traditions can be found in stories about Dionysus, a Greek deity doubling as Bacchus, son of Zeus and Semele; also the cult of the Magna Mata, (the Great Mother) the many-breasted mother goddess Artemis, (twin sister of Apollo, counterpart of Diana) the Celtic god Kernunnos and Tammuz of ancient Sumeria.

Matching elements also exist in the Hindu rites of Vishnu and Shiva, and even the compassion and self-sacrifice displayed in accounts of Jesus Christ.

The Angles and Saxons brought with them to England their protocol of the 'Nerthus' cult of Indo-Germanic pre-history.

Invocation charms of this kind shine a powerful light on how the shamanic agricultural peoples once lived... as the following example shows:

*I pray to the earth and high heaven*

*Erce, erce, erce, Earth Mother.*

*May the almighty Eternal Lord*

*Grant you fields to increase and flourish.*

*Fields fruitful and healthy,*

*Shining harvest of shaft of millet,*

*Broad harvests of barley.*

*Hail to thee, Earth Mother of men.*

*Bring forth now in God's embrace*

*Filled with good for the use of men.*

Lady Raglan's paper about Green Man images within pre-reformation houses of worship, (published by the journal *Folklore*, vol. 50, June 1939, and again by H.M. Carter, *Folklore* vol. 78, winter 1967) bravely defied conventional thinking when observing how 'foliate faces are sometimes the only carving in a church; this attests to their importance, and they appear to be portraits rather than fantasies.'

A Green Man carving from Southwell Minster: Public Domain Image Author: MedievalRich

The distinguished historian had stumbled upon a very ancient message, increasingly recognised regarding its implications for civilisation.

The message is of earth as an organism, a self-regulating system; something that is still taken seriously today in a scientific study called Geophysiology, https://www.youtube.com/watch?v=IB4VXqh9IFs (Geo, earth + physiology, the study of living bodies); this operates under the hypothesis that the planet itself acts as a giant parent organism to all of nature.

I discovered further clues in an extremely well-written work by Stuart Piggott; this book combines fact and folklore when exploring the mysterious history/culture of Celtic priests; his work seeks to give as much insight as possible into the Druids and their world, within the parameters of only a limited amount of archaeological and textual evidence that is available.

*The Druids*, (who were outlawed and largely slaughtered following the Roman conquest of Britain in 43 A.D.) confirms what the Green Man's foliate face is showing us; chiefly, an early fear of, and fascination with, the natural environment; Stuart's book states **'the heart of the forest was the seat of the Godhead, there it displayed its awe; there it saw rites of prayer and magic which propitiated the secret powers of the forest depths and the forest soil; there it claimed humble submission'.**

A dilemma: One might wonder how shamanic man reconciled his awe of nature with his timber requirements – so essential for housing warmth and cooking?

We know that these basic needs were met through considerate land management; such as controlled tree felling, coppicing and pollarding, (for fuel and craft materials) where individual rites of respect were performed before taking the essentials for survival; regular replenishment of the soil, (particularly through the use of earth energy) manuring with excreta, humus, minerals and bone meal, together with Ridge and Furrow gardening.

**In 1908, a privately published book written by the distinguished Montague Fordham, M.A, had this to say: 'We have ignored the teachings of nature and she has had her revenge in the want of fertility of the soil and the deterioration of our national health.'**

That was in 1908, and just imagine the state of our soil now!

We have forgotten that soil is virtually the epidermis of Earth's body.

Anciently, very similar codes of correct planetary respect/conduct are likely to have applied internationally, judging by documentaries set in clay from dynastic Egypt.

Fertility as an energy, was perceived in some countries as being returned to the earth through ritualized dying, (harmless ritualized enactments) and in others by actual sacrifices and rising (s).

Created between the Archaic Kingdom period 2920 BC, (before Khufu... the Great Pyramid and the Old Kingdom 2620 BC) the hieroglyphs record how, if one were going to make a clay pot in those times, one would go to the spot where the clay was to be dug from and pray to the maternal goddess Isis; then humbly, yet earnestly ask her for permission before digging could commence.

Ritualising their woodlands, farmland, sea, and air in a similar manner, they took nothing for granted.

Before the Roman invasion of Britain, oak trees came in for preferential treatment and protection, as these trees were deemed to contain their own personality and were regularly consulted over matters of urgency... as we today might ask a close friend or relative for advice.

For this purpose, Druid priests would interpret the sound of rustling leaves and the tones of wind chimes suspended from branches... a common oracular practise which gave rise to some false notions regarding sacred groves.

In medieval translations of the classics, the term 'sacred grove' is invariably translated 'fidh nemedh' meaning sanctuary; the Irish 'fidh' is equivalent to 'vih' meaning a wood or grove, old Saxon... e.g. as in this description of a *'dense dark, sacred grove which none ordinary dare visit or fell its trees because it was consecrated to the adored gods from the beginning of this world.'*

Planting and maintenance was conducted with fanatical care; where to break a single branch out of malice would result in bad luck for the perpetrator; as this early verse confirms... 'to break an oak branch was deemed a sin; a bad luck job for neighbours – for fire or sickness or the like would mar their honest labours.'

Initially, some may see this as a load of old boloney, but is it really so daft as it first appears? Some latest research informs us that several pieces of work from the U.S. have proven that hugging a tree for 5-10 minutes can help significantly reduce stress levels. Another series of scientifically monitored experiments showed that walking through a forest produced beneficial effects in subjects who suffered from stress.

Was early man so completely naïve when attributing a living soul to plants, inanimate objects, and natural phenomena? Maybe not entirely, just have a look at this feedback about an article in The New Scientist entitled 'Trees may have a 'heartbeat' that is so slow we never noticed it'.

https://twitter.com/newscientist/status/988772763908411393

Veneration of nature can be positively traced back as far as 500 BC, and was practically an international dogma right up until Catholic conversion caused a steady weakening in the once mass practise of Pagan ritual; but to the faithful, tradition always held sway inwardly, affording Green Man and Gaia lasting survival, though in more limited quarters.

This continued to be the case even throughout the effective creation of a commercial, countrywide agricultural landscape.

These damaging times included:

- The indiscriminate destruction of thousands of trees to fuel the thriving Roman iron industry.
- The 'Great Agricultural Revolution' (land privatisation and the introduction of 'Boundary Laws'); Mass land clearances by lordships throughout the financially and politically corrupt periods of Georgian England.
- The massive devastation of British forests throughout the 16th, 17th and 18th centuries, caused by the commercial demand for oak in construction of naval battleships.

In densely populated areas, church investigators successfully dispersed Earth religions during these turbulent ages; though groups elsewhere proved very tenacious and continued-on in secrecy; this feat of survival was achieved by gatherings becoming ever more vigilant and furtive.

In places, the Green Man matured into a conglomerate of intertwining concepts.

He began to be considered as an elemental consort to earth – 'the preferred creatrix'.

In other parts, Gaia and Green Man became hybridised with ancient Sun-God observances – a subject strictly requiring a separate edition altogether.

The proliferation of uncovered clues points to one common denominator binding all camps of earth worshippers throughout the ages firmly together; namely, an obsession with the geometrical alignment of sacred fertility sites.

There is clearly an elemental and biological need deep-rooted within, urging many of us to address our special need for a long-lost common sense; however, the tacky consumer trivialisations that we 'enjoy' today cannot entirely satiate this subconscious hunger.

**The Buried God**

In the West, our discussed Earth Deities the Green Man and Gaia, (earth mother and sky father) were associated with Sacred Groves containing the mighty *oak, at which votive offerings would be buried in their honour.*No doubt that one reason for the popularity of the Oak in Pagan philosophy was the Phallic likeness of its acorn fruit.

'Grove' has its roots in Old English, hailing from 'Graf' and 'Grafan', meaning 'to dig'.

It originally denoted 'an alley cut in a wooded area for purposes of worship'; though all the while, enormous efforts were being made to debauch the word, so that it progressively became associated with darkness and pessimism; as exhibited in Kings 23. v14 of the Bible, 'and he broke in pieces the images and cut down the groves and filled their places with the bones of man.'

By using jaundiced promotions like this, (especially in the Bible) it became quite easy for our controllers to twist positive expressions and make them synonymous in the public mind with death and negativity.

A one-off perhaps? Hardly!

Belated adaptations and revisions of Biblical narrative under the order of a particular ruler, (whether that be King James or whoever) would have provided the perfect opportunity for the insertion of specific word mechanisms; a branch of psychological manipulation that can be traced back as far as ancient Greece.

Sociological Modification is what it was all about, a practise that has become even more commonplace today, particularly in the word-handling of political propaganda and advertising.

A good example in this context is the word 'Learning'; Look how in essence we view 'Learning' as being synonymous with 'Earning'. For it won't have escaped your notice these days, how University 'education' is now almost exclusively marketed as 'the key to future job careers'; and only rarely, (if at all) as **wisdom for the enrichment of one's mind and character** – as it used to be.

To those who still fail to accept this, just think about what happens should anyone overstep the bounds of societal acceptability – then they are said to be 'out of control'; meaning that the person in discussion, (prior to them going 'out of control') previously was under a type of state jurisdiction, (as we all are) before they decided to break with convention and community rules and become an individual.

As with most things in our carefully engineered existence, look too closely and it will be noticed how first impressions are sometimes rubbish; things aren't always what they seem; something which yet again, is the total reverse to what religious and educational processing has taught us.

The Roman invaders, (those master indoctrinators) can be partly blamed for our state of unawareness today.

The irony of these guys, is that while they were *getting-off* spreading misinformation about our terrible heathen lifestyles, they hadn't even put their own house in order first; because at this time, most hypocritical Romans were still paying homage to 'Bacchus', a variant image of the Green Man himself!

He was a character who, complete with leafy face, was the Greek god of Wine and Ecstasy; and from this connection we see an expansion of 'Bacchus' into the botanical terms *Bacciferous* = 'a plant bearing berries', *Bacciform*, (shaped like a berry) and so it goes on, until in the 16th century when we arrive at the title for a plant species called N. tabacum or 'Tobacco'... taken from Spanish 'tabaco', with its informal name of 'Baccy'.

My foregoing examples serve to illustrate the prime importance of etymological research in relation to estimating our true heritage; the recovery of past customs which are often conserved in the most innocuous-looking words of everyday language.

I find it so amusing, that whenever there is a programme on the TV about British archaeology/history... it is nearly always about the bloody Romans!

It's an almost predictable script, as we're consistently reminded just how wonderful and clever they were; and yes, the Roman's really did teach us Brits a thing or two... principally about divide and rule, as they proceeded to separate our little island into Borough's, tax us to the hilt and govern folk accordingly, coming down hard on as much of our traditional ways as possible.

I imagine some people might cite Roman building prowess as some kind of defence. What about roads? the Roman's gave us roads? I hear them cry.

So, what about them? would be my reply.

I've no doubt that we had some decent and well-trodden routes long before *they* invaded; and it is likely that the Romans simply surfaced over many of those.

And I have no doubt that they played a part in physically vandalising our major sacred sites as well; just consider one of the fallen lintels at Stonehenge, (mysteriously having been dislodged with force from its mortise and tenon fitting) and one can easily envisage a few daring centurions somehow clambering 30 feet up there to lever-off and topple the huge cross stone.

The lintels were held in place with mortise and tenon joints; the tenon was carved on top of the standing sarsen and the mortise hole carved into the lintel; this allowed them to join together like Lego bricks!

How much do you reckon such *megalithic maniacs* would have been rewarded by their captain? at least several silver pieces for so much backbreaking effort surely!

Guidebooks inform us that an earthquake probably felled this and several other stones there anciently; really? I can't imagine we ever had quakes powerful enough in this country to move 25 Ton stones!

'The Professionals' eh, don't you just love them?

On November 27, 2007, I joined the US History Channel team who visited Stonehenge, Wiltshire, UK, to be filmed conducting certain dowsing experiments for a television documentary that they were making relating to the connection between Ley Lines, Earth Energies and UFOs.

For reference, I took along with me some extremely rare VHS footage that was originally shot at Stonehenge in 1990 by record producer David Tickle.

Early in 2008, the finished documentary called 'UFO Vortexes', (part of The UFO Hunters series) was screened.

The David Tickle video clip featured on this programme appears to show the manifestation of an aerial light form, whilst also revealing at the same time a variety of objects which are seen emerging out of a nearby ancient burial mound, as if in harmony with the UFO appearance.

Although the footage is quite grainy by modern-day standards, (at that time 22 years old, and transferred from VHS to digital) it is my belief that the artefacts seen popping up from the mound are not flaws or other problems with the analogue videotape, (as sceptic's have argued) but are what I believe to be the first visual evidence of Ley Energy to have been captured on film.

It is said that the sprawling monument of Stonehenge and its surrounding sacred sites are all positioned on crisscrossing Ley Lines, (also called Geo Energy lines).

Now just a wreck of its former majesty, yet still this location attracts mysterious phenomena from time-to-time; today it's subtle, but just imagine what it was like here when new!

Built with mathematical precision by lost civilizations, some of these places seem to be home to naturally occurring 'window areas' which 'open' under certain conditions, thus allowing strange spectacles to become manifest.

Through my private researches, I have also noticed that wherever these 'places of power' exist, important military establishments are also to be found within a few miles or so of them.

Is there a connection, or is it just a remarkable concurrence of circumstances?

Please decide for yourselves.

www.beamsinvestigations.org/07-05-
1990%20UFO%20Earth%20Energies%20Captured%20on%20Video%20Stoneheng
e,%20Wilts.html

Any scholar who believes that they can fathom the manner and intent of first-
time rites purely from modern-day history literature is deceiving himself or
herself.

Late medieval satires and the eulogies can be highly misleading also; for even
then, customs had undergone numerous phases of cultural metamorphosis,
starting with the Romanisation of Britain.

Take this poignant reminder of how the ideology of Britons has changed in just a
couple of hundred years.

Since Georgian times, the British May Queen, (Latin Maius, French Maia = the
goddess of growth) celebrations declined from one of the major 'Holy Daies' in
our calendar into what is now a Bank HOLIDAY; so, from a sacred holy day to a
commercial holiday... a bit of a downturn there.

Man's indigenous knowledge has clearly become corrupted; yet even from the
salvaged debris of Pagan generations we have been able to make strong progress
in testing our suspicions, enabling us to reconstruct these mysterious times in
print.

Rather than eradicating every trace of primal worship though, certain Pagan philosophies were cunningly incorporated INTO Christian doctrine by doing such things as integrating Pagan iconography like the Green Man... canonising the Pagan water goddess 'Brigid', (which is where we get the word 'bridge' from) or 'Brid', (another of Gaia's superintendents) into 'Saint Bridget', and converting fertility springs into Baptismal Wells at every given opportunity.

Robert Hunter's *Encyclopaedic Dictionary*, (1894) and Jeffrey Kacirck's *Forgotten English,* (Pomegranate books) reveal how those in power would do anything to achieve their aims.

In 1564, amongst the assorted rules of suppression already in place at that time, the church's council appointed a commission to compile a list of forbidden books.

The result was the *index-prohibitorum*, a published 'register of books which may not be read by Roman Catholics, cleric or the lay' on pain of ex-communication.

Livy 39:16 testifies to the practice of burning books of magic in pagan Rome, and how the Ephesian converts who used 'curious arts', voluntarily did the same, (Act 19:19).

Prior to the invention of printing there were many cases in which Roman pontiffs had suppressed the writing of authors whom they had judged as heretical.

Ever wondered about the ancient burning of the Great University of Alexandria?

This is where Christian monks under Theophilus, torched an estimated 150,000 priceless works of Science, Philosophy, Religion and Occult Matters, together with a 30-volume compilation of Egyptian temple records.

Precisely what prohibited knowledge of ancestral genius were they trying to conceal from mankind?

Back home again, and try testing more words phonetically, then you will soon see that other common terms, not necessarily found associated with place names, such as 'Alley', (a Ley) 'Lane', (Leyne) etc... and expressions like 'Lie of the Land', (Ley of the Land?) may also have a role to play in our search criteria.

Erstwhile NASA scientist, Maurice Chatelain has revealed what he sees as an exclusive control situation by the foremost religions, and that The Vatican secretly holds a 'Sacred Codex' which could reveal the truth about Mans origins and former beliefs.

It is wondered also, what other important works, (perhaps individual books rescued prior to the decimation at Alexandria) are also preserved in their private vaults?

Remember, we are not concerned with the elitist classes 'version' of history, (deliberately veiled his-story, the story according to whichever ruler happened to be in power at any given time) here, we are attempting to rediscover our OWN original Pagan belief systems and roots.

## Holy Alignments

Please let me say before I tell you more about my findings, I am getting rather fed up with coming across a certain type of site on the internet; the sort whose sole aim is to downplay the subjects of Gaia, Ley Lines, Earth Energies, Lost Advanced Civilizations and UFOs.

I've examined quite a few of these and find it curious how they all seem to be composed in a similar manner; initially, such material takes on the appearance of being fairly objective and may even give some signs of encouragement... as if to catch the reader's attention; but then, like a roller coaster, the piece rapidly takes a big nose dive into negativity land.

I just don't understand - how could these people have got things so wrong?

I suspect this type of material is either being written by naive graduate-types with no practical knowledge of what they are condemning, (likely enough basing their presentations on the unfounded opinions of professional sceptics and science textbook bias) or worse, certain agencies are attempting to control, manipulate, and warp public opinion.

Ley Lines, (a title coined only last century and much misused since through new age ideologies) are to be found all over the world; yet they are only partially discernible by way of their landscape alignment marker points; or, if these have been lost/buried through time, development etc, the markers may still be detectable either through the careful research of historical records, Etymology (the study of place names... and as I warned just now, be very, very careful with your reference sources) maps and also by dowsing.

Likely to have been laid out under the guidance of geomancers, these great achievements of surveying resemble a sort of roughly linear dot-to-dot puzzle.

They are comprised of sacred sites which were built at intervals in relatively neat lines, in areas that have literally been saturated by thousands of years of devotional energy.

Personally speaking, I would say that Ley Lines had multiple uses; primarily as cult ceremonial, processional, pilgrimage routes... with others also doubling as the quickest way to travel across the countryside from A to B!

There are times though when conventional Ley Line principle gives the impression of temporary abandonment, as alignments become quite broad, leaving instead jagged features in the building arrangement, with various curves, kinks and detours along the way, before eventually resuming back on track.

My feeling is that this type of apparent occasional disorder may have been deliberate, with leys possibly following the pattern of underground water flows, which obviously do not themselves always travel evenly.

The lines often criss-cross to form giant isosceles triangles and other interesting geometry, stretching across the countryside, ranging from two or three miles in length and beyond.

It is believed that certain lines may even be of primordial, ritualistic solar significance, as at solstice or equinox.

Where two or more Ley Lines cross, the intersection point is often known as a Ley Node or Nexus.

Often included along each line are: Medieval churches and their more modern counterparts; abbey's, castles, (as many of the pre-Reformation sanctuaries, abbey's etc were built on the sites of *Pagan temples) earthen landscape effigies, stone megaliths, artificial mounds, funerary locations... along with other important features in the landscape such as springs, wells and groves; all of these, (whether still standing and preserved, crumbling remnants or simply the long-buried foundations of) can be classed as elements which constitute a Ley Line. *'Temples once made with the boughs of trees should now be turned into churches'. 'This way the pleasures once permitted to the English country folk, in connection with places familiar from their earliest remembrances can be associated with their new belief.' *Sulpicius*

**Who Laid Out The Leys?**

It might seem quite absurd to most in this high-tech age, the concept of primeval burial mounds, standing stones and churches having been constructed, (often thousands of years apart) with some kind of mystical connecting ritual in mind... lines spanning in all points of the compass across the world; yet this idea is precisely what dozens of very influential pioneers have suggested.

The problem is of course, how could the ley system have been achieved thousands of years ago - and who made it?

Here is one idea, first publicized in 1922.

Council representative and originator of the photographic exposure meter, Alfred Watkins, (1855-1935) usually had a sensible and practical attitude towards life based on these merits; yet here was a realist who then furthered his list of achievements by becoming noted as 'rediscoverer of the ritual landscape alignment'.

He personally believed that the 226ft tall, prehistoric turf-cut figure in Sussex known as the Long Man of Wilmington, depicts the type of individual responsible for such alignments; it shows what could well be an ancient priest/surveyor holding his two measuring staves or rods.

According to Mr Watkins, the names 'Dod-Man' or alternatively 'Rod-Man', are but two titles worth looking out for when examining the origin and historical development of words and their meanings.

I think that the 'Dod' idea does have some merit to our particular investigations, yet its meaning is somewhat confusing; having said that, it could be related to the word 'hod', meaning 'an open box attached to a long pole handle'; as in a brick hod, a three-sided box for carrying bricks or other building materials, often mortar; [and here I am envisioning church construction... see where I am

coming from with this?

When visiting churches, monuments etc, look out for surveyor's and stonemasons' marks, often left on walls, like the ones in this picture - along with other designs. These obscure symbols are to be found, not only on churches, but other building constructions such as bridges, all-round this country. We may walk past them without given these symbols a second glance. They are usually chiselled into the stone and are supposed to represent an arrow pointing up from below a horizontal line. Strange how they also resemble Ley Lines going to a horizon point!

Despite standard history books hardly helping us at all to pursue further evidence about this matter, I get the impression that some of our native Geomancers were more than likely known as 'Rod-Men', or something similar according to location; the proof being that a few records specifically use that name.

Plural: Rod Men: A Rodman is a person who carries the levelling rod in surveying.

Noun: One who carries and employs a levelling rod under the supervision of a surveyor.

The rod or perch or pole is a surveyor's tool and its unit of length is exactly equal to 5 1/2 yards, 16 1/2 feet, 1/320 of a statute mile or one-fourth of a surveyor's chain (approximately 5.0292 meters). The rod is useful as a unit of length because whole number multiples of it can form one acre of square measure.

The term 'Rod' also turns up in researches about bygone surveying practices and is closely related to the old Saxon 'roda' and old Norse word 'rotha'.

The idea is that Rodmen would have laid out the whole network, generation after generation, using calibration staves, hazel divining rods, intuitive powers, and various earth incantations.

Over time, these experts on topography and triangulation, would carefully assess angles, altitudes, and distances, before setting out on the ground the position of each proposed component construction at an appropriate interval from its neighbour.

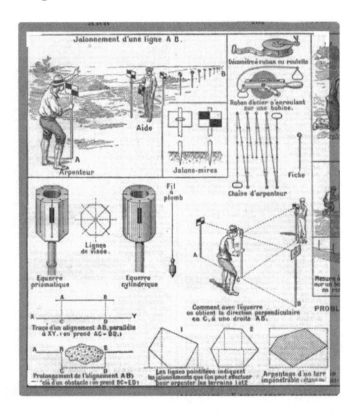

Before aerial photography became commonplace, trigonometry points would have been manually set out at various stages across the landscape using basic surveying equipment and intuition.

There is much to indicate that these early feats of surveying really happened, not just here in Britain, but globally, with groups of dedicated shamans from many countries working in collaboration. A trans-European grid network could have eventually been formed with alignments of ritual sites encompassing the world, spanning from Avebury, Wilts, England, to the Great Pyramid of Giza, Egypt, from Angkor Wat, Cambodia to Stanton Drew, Somerset, England!

Surveying the lay of the land was popular in Europe around the 5th century, as this period engraving shows.

I have conducted quite a bit of research on the Rod-Man theory, particularly in connection with English place names, and here are a few interesting examples I have uncovered that contain the 'Rod' syllable in their titles.

Please study the following history snippets carefully: Note the interesting ancient earthworks/other likely ley marker sites and potential leads about their Pagan background that these places all contain. It is magnificent to think how these word clues survived the ravages of suppression when some other important Pagan memories enjoyed only a brief recorded existence by comparison.

**Rodborough**, Stroud, Gloucestershire: The name of the parish is originally that of an Iron Age earthwork on Rodborough common, and is recorded from the 8th century; the derivation of the first part of the name is uncertain, but it may derive from a clearing in the woodland which anciently covered much of Minchinhampton and Rodborough commons.

**Rodmarton**, Gloucestershire: Evidence of a Roman settlement has been found at Rodmarton. Through the parish runs a Roman trackway from Cirencester and Chavenage Green, adjacent to which is a long barrow; also known as a chambered tomb, the long barrow is a style of monument that was constructed across Western Europe in the fifth and fourth millennia BCE, during the Early Neolithic period. These were typically constructed from earth and either timber or stone, the oldest and most widespread methods of construction in the world.

Rodmarton has its church dedicated to St. Peter, which stands sentinel over the village as a powerful testimonial to the continuity of the Christian faith. In general terms it is a Norman church, but no one really knows how old it is.

A priest is recorded in 1086, Samuel Lysons - nephew of the famous antiquary, who thought there were traces of a heathen temple on the site of the present church; and F. W. Parkinson, (Rector 1913-1940) tells us 'when the wall of the west end of the church, being in a dangerous state, was opened for repairs in 1926, the remains of a Celtic Cross were discovered with interlacing carving; no doubt this cross had formed part of a Saxon church and had been used for rebuilding in Norman times'.

**Rodden**, Somerset: Records show that its church was only built in 1640, but more importantly, it stands on the site of an earlier medieval church.

**Rode**, Somerset: It's church, St Lawrence dates from the late 14th and early 15th century and was constructed on the site of an earlier ecclesiastical building. The village appears as 'Rode' in the Domesday Book, but its spelling was taken from the early word 'Roda', meaning clearing.

**Rodhuish Common**, Somerset: An Iron Age Earthwork enclosure, (range 1200 B.C. and 600 B.C) situated on Rodhuish Common, 300m west of Moor Barn.

It is one of a number of similarly constructed enclosures which occupy hillslopes in the locality. As far as I can tell, any detailed environmental evidence and archaeological reports concerning the purpose of the enclosure, its inhabitants, and the landscape in which they lived, are lacking.

**Rodney Stoke**, Somerset: Close to the village is Westbury Camp, which represents the remains of an <u>Iron Age enclosed settlement</u> and has been designated as a Scheduled Ancient Monument. The 'Stoke' part of its title is a bit of a red herring from our point of view, in that it merely means 'a stockaded settlement' from the Old English 'stoc'.

Clearly though, it isn't just 'Rod' that we must concern ourselves with; there are a plethora of other revealing syllables forming the whole or part of place names that require investigation; in this book I have tried to list as many as I can, but in reality, to cover this comprehensively would require several lifetimes.

Further pointers to watch out for are places whose chronicles contain quaint legends, fictitious monster lore, maybe of a giant slithering snake such as the Shervage Wurm

https://www.britainexpress.com/counties/somerset/churches/crowcombe.htm

of Somerset, (watch out for the variant Old English spellings) a local knight who becomes the fearless beastie slayer, and of course, a helpless maiden who is rescued from the jaws of death by our stereotypical hero in shining armour.

Such inherited stories are, I am certain, Christian victory over Paganism propaganda; rather like St. George supposedly slaying the dragon in the 12th century and St. Patrick, the Christian missionary, who purportedly rid Ireland of snakes during the fifth century A.D.

In the Middle Ages, dragon and snake iconography were said to have been commonly employed by the church to represent Evil; and whenever a pocket of cultural earth worship tradition could be diluted, and its cult members converted to Christianity... then that is how these fireside stories were doubtless born.

Conversely, perhaps unbeknown to the Church, dragons and snakes were also believed by Pagans to represent the shapely flows of Gaia's aquiferous arterial system!

**The dragon; simple mythology or a secret symbol for the curvilinear flow of subterranean energy?**

Witchcraft, fairies and that type of folk memory... can also be coloured reminiscences about the former magical beliefs and practises of an area.

Whilst hardly achieving national pastime status, over the years – and mainly thanks to Alfred Watkins, 'Ley Hunting' slowly began to attain more and more in the way of public credibility.

Regional enthusiast's clubs began to be formed dedicated to finding ancient alignments, with its map-addicted members combing the countryside.

As time wore on, more radical ideas started to be bandied about within the subject; and it wasn't long before old-style thinkers took a back seat as fresh devotees overhauled the entire Straight Track benchmark.

Recumbent Sarsen stones at Farnborough Hill, School

Please see this report of a very interesting ley alignment that I have discovered, walked, dowsed, and monitored intently... part of which is shown in the above picture.

http://www.beamsinvestigations.org/FARNBOROUGH%20-%20A%20Mini%20Stonehenge1.html

A contemporary of Watkins lived in Germany.

Nowhere near as conservative as his British counterpart, clergyman Wilhelm Teudt...

https://en.wikipedia.org/wiki/Wilhelm_Teudt

... (1860 - 1942) dubbed these connections of sacred sites as 'Holy Lines' or 'Heilige Linien' - and charted dozens of examples stretching for miles across the 'fatherland.'

His findings were published in Germanische Heiigtumer 1929 but quickly rejected by experts shortly after; yet they still have some influence in Germany today.

Another worthwhile piece of information is the patronization of Teudts' work by Karl Haushofer, occultic advisor to Adolf Hitler.

There is testimonial about Haushofer helping construct certain Third Reich sites on earth energy hotspots.

Other direct proof exists, that both pre and post war Germany were quite advanced in their exploration of tellurian fields.

For instance, in Die Welt Der Geheimen Machte, (The World of Secret Forces, a book written by Siegfried Wittman, Austria in 1952) it is suggested how the surface of the earth is formed from a grid system of positive and negative forces.

Based on the researches of Professor Dr George Anschutz, Dr Theol, Dr Hubert, J Urban and Professor Helmut Wolf, the plan was proven to abide by strict mathematical co-ordinates corresponding to known geodetic data.

Further to this, other evidence that I have come across indicates that specific churches, circular/ovoid megalithic edifices and single stones, may have even been architecturally designed to be harmonically tuned to a certain reception frequency, and further refined by adding, smoothing, sculpting and angling until the correct effect was achieved.

**Where Has the Power Gone?**

These days it is important not to expect all Ley Lines to be highly energetic anymore; a phenomenon known as 'crustal shift' must be considered.

This is where divisions of earth's lithosphere, or exterior surface, (otherwise termed as the 'crust') is imperceptibly slipping all the while; we might only be discussing fractions of an inch per year, but over long periods of time, the accumulative effects are considerable; and whilst these vast rafts of land are gradually moving in this manner, earth's core obviously stays put.

What this means is, after all these centuries there has been so much lithospheric movement, that many arrangements of ley markers will be severely out of station with the earth's magnetic flows and thus not working correctly as once they undoubtedly did; a mere shadow of their former glory.

Still, a 'shadow' is better than nothing, and I can vouch for the fact that miniscule trickles of energy are continuing to get through in places, detectable by dowsing...

and felt through the body sometimes; not so much as a high-power shock, more the mild tingle one would get if you were to put your tongue on the terminals of a small, run down 9v battery.

I know, I have felt the power myself sometimes, trickling through me and even beneath my feet, most notably at St Laurence, Seale, Surrey... an interesting old church founded in 1080 that is certainly worth checking out. (including energies that are possibly Aquiferous in origin.)

This has been known to cause a sense of disorientation in some people.

As you can see, the Seale church stands on a significant ley alignment.

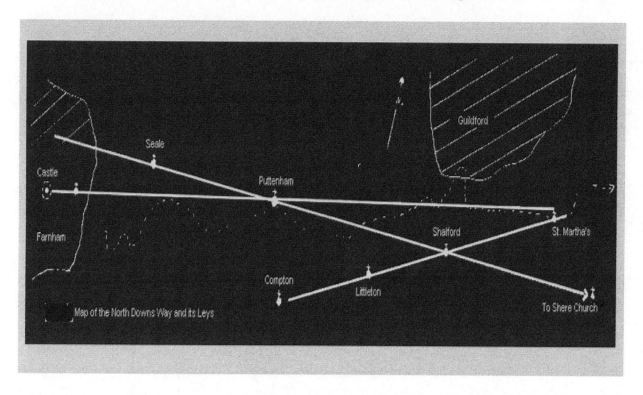

Marshalling all the evidence together, makes clear the potential magnitude of what we are considering here... a living circuit of Bioenergetic Current or 'Yunni' as the Celts used to call it... now damaged by both nature itself and mankind's handiwork.

It may take the wind out of some readers sails to learn that the Catholic church definitely flirted with the occult, whose religious buildings, contrary to popular belief, often displayed signs of the Zodiac and other Magical symbols)

https://blog.medicinegarden.com/2011/06/zodiac-signs-in-a-catholic-church/

because Astrology was an accepted science throughout the church from as far back as 595, right up until the 17th century!

There are lots of words still in general usage today that illustrate this early belief in Astral Influences... such as 'Disaster', (note the phonetics DIS-AS-STER or STAR) which signals the unpropitious aspects of a particular star, (itself, a word derived from the Latin 'Astrum'); and perhaps the ultimate piece of word puffery is 'Terror' – meaning 'great fear or dread', which directly originates from the Latin 'Terra' = earth or land!

With such an obvious interest in occult matters, it has to be wondered could the Ley Grid system have been known about by the church hierarchy back then?

My suspicions were further raised when I learned how Pope Gregory 590 to 604 AD, specifically instructed Augustine and his fellow 40 missionaries, (who were sent to the Anglo-Saxon kingdom of Kent and other districts in an attempt to convert the Pagan Anglo-Saxon to Christianity) NOT to destroy the ancient Pagan marker sites there due to their special importance, but rather, convert the shrines to Christian usage.

A very good example of such a Pagan/church 'marriage', can be found at The St Mary's Church Eversley, Hampshire.

## Pagan Stone Beneath Altar Floor 'Mystery'

St Mary's, Eversley, Hampshire, a place of worship for over 900 years

From late antiquity and throughout the Middle Ages, Pagan sites were invariably Christianized in some way.

This was first achieved through church hype, publicly condemning Pagan temples and practices; next came the demolition of pre-Christian establishments - then the erection of buildings for Christian worship directly over their foundations.

Yet things were not always as clear cut as this; there is evidence to suggest that those who controlled the churches' governing structure were split over the Christianization of sites, and that concessions were sometimes made to Paganism; this included the incorporation of earth worship iconography in churches, such as foliate man... decorative carvings in stone and upon wooden bench ends; but sometimes it seems, on rare occasions, an even greater compromise was struck;

this involved ancient standing stones deliberately being left in situ during the construction of churchyards - and even more bizarrely, sometimes being incorporated into the very fabric of churches!

Effectively, this practice was 'permitted' in order to attract Pagan folk away from their traditional customs of worshiping stones and trees, and persuading them to go into these shiny new edifices called churches; but maybe there was also an element of superstition going on here by the architects; and dare we say it - even some clerics who may have had a soft spot for nature worship beliefs.

This mix of Christian and Pagan within early churches is certainly not an uncommon phenomenon, and one superb example can be found at St Mary's, Eversley, Hampshire, England.

Beneath a secreted hatch in the floor right by the font, there exists an ancient megalith! It's as if St Mary's has been built around this Sarsen stone - yet it is kept hidden... why?

A Pagan standing stone in the floor by a Christian font!

Interesting, considering how originally, sarsen standing stones were of as much sacred importance to the Pagans as the later church fonts were to Christians.

Almost as if it is being kept secret, a rug is usually placed over the hatch; but one only has to lift this to reveal a wooden compartment; pull out the two loose slats, raise the lid and you will find a deep recess in the floor which encases the sarsen megalith.

Although only the top is visible, it is a truly stunning sight - from our point of view anyway; probably most these days wouldn't give two hoots.

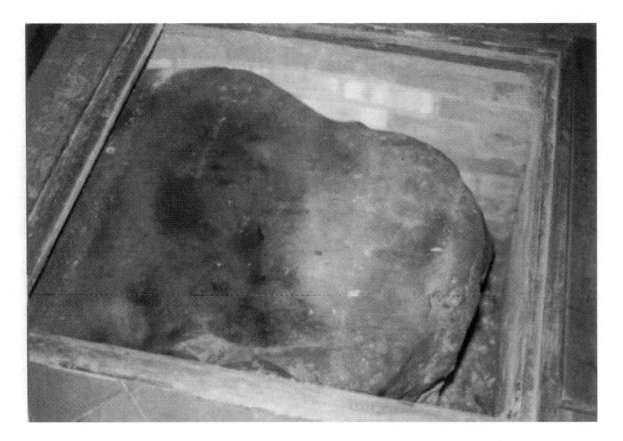

Top of the ancient stone revealed - which probably has more again below ground as on display here

The stone is often wet to the touch or even has a small water puddle on it - a combination of dampness from the ground, exacerbated no doubt by a stream that runs just a short walk away from here.

Despite its somewhat glossy appearance in the photo, in fact there is no glass covering this stone.

Of course, just as with most visitors to standing stone circle sites, the natural desire is to touch the megalith and feel its wonderful cold, aged surface; was this the idea perhaps? physical contact between human and stone?

It isn't difficult to imagine 'private' rituals going on here when the church was closed-off to local folk.

Old habits dying hard?

Notice the accumulation of water on the stone? Strange coincidence this, seeing as how the baptismal font is situated so close to where the stone lies hidden away.

Reasoning for the stone's dankness quickly becomes clear when exploring outside – as a tiny, but distinguished tributary, issuing from the River Blackwater, is discovered trickling several hundred yards away; 'distinguished' because its iron-rich waters are the colour of BLOOD!

The sarsen could be acting like a sponge.

This all might seem like madness in our digital age, but people once held great store in nature and superstition; and to look at this another way, perhaps early beliefs were no more daft than us believing everything we see and hear on TV today, as some people do.

For instance, it was once even believed that nettles gathered on sanctified soil and boiled down for a drink, had the power to cure various ailments; and similarly, the dew gathered from graveyards was considered highly efficacious against specific maladies.

Just a couple of hundred years ago, water taken from a small stream or a brook was considered to be 'water from the living earth'; water sources were known as 'bournes' - as in born from the earth.

Complete balderdash one might think, but who are we to say that such 'quack' cures and beliefs are wrong and ineffective?

As with the supposed power of prayer, the power of belief might merely be a case of attempting to exert mind over matter... but as we all know, sometimes miracles of faith do happen!

Hilary and myself have dowsed this church and its grounds, and we can verify that our L-shape dowsing rods came alive here several times; the strongest reaction we found being around the main entrance, the stone itself, middle of the church and its altar.

Eversley's importance in the Pagan scheme of things, is further strengthened by a bronze-age bowl barrow called Cudbury Clump, located on Eversley Upper Common.

The Bronze Age 'bowl barrow', overgrown and surrounded by a tree-ring. (Creative Commons image]

A word of caution here; small rural churches like this used to be open most days, but now, due to cutbacks and a spate of thefts, they are kept locked more often than not, and are usually only open for maintenance, baptisms, weddings and funerals.

We discovered this stone by sheer accident a few years back when randomly visiting St Mary's as part of our researches, and as luck would have it, there was nobody else around; and me being the curious person that I am, it was a case of what's under the rug? and upon finding this little set-up, taking a chance and photographing everything before replacing the boards and rug back to normal as quickly as possible - just in case anyone should suddenly walk in; although I'm sure if one were to seek permission first it would be granted... that is, if you can track down the vicar!

While examining my map sheet, I noticed that next in line, (just 3 miles away) is St. Peter's Church, Yateley.

I mused over whether the two churches could have any interesting connections historically, so I conducted another round of archival delving; and, after wading through a few *waste of time* pages about Yateley on the net... suddenly I hit pay dirt as I discovered what I would call a Ley hunter's dream come true!

St. Peter's Church, Yateley, Hampshire in 1909

Quite frankly, this is the last place that I would have expected to find evidence of, (what is for us anyway) the Holy Grail of admissions… on the church's own website! The 'history' page of St Peter's church Yateley makes a fascinating mention: *'The doorway in the porch is a good example of early Norman work, it is made of chalk. The heavy door was burnt on the inside but has been expertly restored by local craftsmen. Between the inner and outer doors is a panel displaying a map of the church before and after the fire. The porch is typical of those built around 1450. It was undamaged in the fire. The stone walls were inserted during the last century, probably in 1878.* **_On either side of the Porch, just visible at ground level, are ancient "sarsen" stones, probably once an upright Pagan circle, but flattened to form the foundations of the Christian church'._**

Pagan Sarsen stone remnant jutting out

That direct quote, (a very rare admission from an ecclesiastical source) surely begs an important question; just how many other towns and villages across Britain once boasted their own stone circles and Pagan shrines etc, only for them to be mindlessly vandalized... smashed and removed as society was steadily re-engineered by our religious and political leaders, then had churches put in their place?

Now we turn our attention to the place name of Yateley; the title *Yateley* derives from the Middle English 'Yate' meaning 'Gate', (into Windsor Forest) and 'Lea' which was a 'forest clearing'. Although in historic records variants of the spelling include 'Hyatele', 'Yateleghe', 'Yatche', 'Yatelighe', 'Yeatley', 'Yeateley'.

Reading this literally, we have either a 'gate' into the forest... [a very obvious walking route from Yateley to Eversley and beyond to who knows what other sacred sites and structures - with some likely having been levelled countless years ago, built over etc] or 'gate to the 'ley line'; either way, both potentially relating to a ceremonial pathway of a bygone religion - the worship of earth and all its mysteries.

The main interior of this church has been converted; the altar is now partitioned-off from what is in effect a big hall, that, according to the notices I studied, holds regular get togethers, craft fairs and various exhibitions.

A vulgar design to my eyes, but the locals that I watched milling about the place, (many of whom were more fixated with their mobiles than looking around them), seem happy enough with it.

Being a traditionalist myself, I would call it disappointing; the outside though is a different matter; look closely and there are still a few tell-tale signs of our true heritage to be discovered amidst the renovation work.

I first visited this church years ago, and on my recent return I found that a lot has changed; I don't remember it like it is now; apart from what has happened within, I recall when I was there last that I explored a really long, (and I mean REALLY long) very old, dead-straight pathway that ran for over a mile or so behind the church; today I find this partially lost, apparently due to various commercial developments and having been replaced by more up-to-date footpaths.

Local historian Arthur E Lunn, who I had an interesting chat with before he later sadly passed away, suggested to me that *heavy sarsens from the Surrey Ridge could have been placed upon log rafts, floated down the deep, sluggish Blackwater River and dragged* to the once venerated sites around Hampshire.

Most Ley Lines also served as pathways for Pilgrims who travelled across country between these sites of holy significance; from what I have studied, there was a definite belief in bygone centuries that walking the lines, (for miles on end sometimes) served to purify oneself, while at the same time creating a deeper connection with the Living Earth/God.

Contrary to what some critics say, I believe there is much more to Ley Lines than mere coincidence of positioning as 'they' would have us believe; but why not decide by becoming a Ley Quester yourself?

**Why Not Embark Upon Your Own Personal Quest?**

To do this you need to begin by purchasing two types of Ordnance Survey paper map: a Landranger, (1:50,000 scale) and a copy of the more detailed Pathfinder series, (1:25,000 scale). It is advisable to consult your stockist about the 'title' you would prefer, as each area is covered by a separate sheet number.

You also need a transparent ruler, a sharp pencil, and a rubber.

While bearing in mind that the sacral ways would have undoubtedly determined the positioning of virtually every branch of communal life, one should start by using the Landranger map to search for consistencies in the placement of ancient sites.

On average, a 'Ley Line' would be defined as five or more aligned sacred sites, spanning over a distance not exceeding 4 miles, before that in itself would connect to another on the grid… taking into account of course, that today much has disappeared, become lost and built upon.

Recalling the clever site continuity carried out by clerical authorities with their construction of pre-reformation buildings upon Pagan ground… historical revered places to search for on your map should include; those marked 'Place of Worship' or 'Former Place of Worship', (these may involve 'church', 'abbey', 'cathedral', 'priory', 'monastery' and 'chapel')

| ✦ | Place of worship |
|---|---|

Current or former place of worship;

| ▲ | with tower |
|---|---|
| ▲ | with spire, minaret or dome |

Look out also for 'motte', 'bailey', 'earthwork', 'henge', 'mound', and 'tumulus', (tumuli)… marked **'visible earthwork'** in *Gothic font. *When you see a gothic label on the map, it means the site is archaeological, but one that isn't Roman. The feature will usually be prehistoric, (i.e. before AD43) or medieval, (from the 400 AD mark until around 1600) or slightly later.

Don't ignore castles either, as invariably these were raised on former ancient foundations which could have been anything, with many strongholds also housing their own chapels.

Also key in our quest are 'wells' and 'springs', (marked 'W' or 'Spr') possibly anything termed as a 'site of antiquity' and wayside 'monuments', (marked 'Mon' or by a bold cross) with all of these abbreviations and symbols dependant on the age of your map.

| ✤ | Site of antiquity | **VILLA** | Roman | ∗ ⸬⸬ | Visible earthwork |
|---|---|---|---|---|---|
| ⚔ 1066 | Site of battle (with date) | Castle | Non-Roman | | |

Please be extremely cautious when using place names ending in the 'ley' syllable for guidance.

While a number of these might be worthy of consideration in your search, many are too wide-ranging in their meaning and do not always fix a precise geographical spot, date, and intent of first land usage.

Alfred Watkins coined the term 'ley' for one good reason... the high incidence of British place appellations ending with the 'ley' syllable which seemed to occur in abundance along these measured ways.

There is little doubt that our man had a point, but scholars of earth mysteries must beware of falling into a potentially fatal trap here.

Post Doomsday Book treatises cite the Anglo-Saxon word 'ley' as denoting either a 'field', 'fallow land', 'a glade' or a 'woodland clearing.'

Paradoxically, much senior tradition expands the list of meanings for 'ley' as 'church paths', 'monolithic stones' and 'earthen mounds.'

These differences in meaning serve to illustrate just how complicated the subject of place name research can be... so, proceed with caution!

Putting all of these factors into context, as far as clues towards our rediscovery of the specially engineered terrain of Ley Lines, it can now be seen that only in exceptional circumstances should the 'ley' syllable, (along with its many variants 'lay', 'lea', 'lee', 'leigh' etc) be counted as evidence.

Any significant shortfalls when hunting for ley sites on maps might be solved by consulting the more comprehensive Pathfinder sheet, where the searcher may be fortunate enough to locate additional pointers... smaller sites not covered by the 1:50,000 scale maps.

Record your map discoveries in the form of a connecting pencil line through each straight, (or relatively so) row of sites.

If you are able, try physically walking as much of each line as it is still possible to do, soaking up the atmosphere as you go.

Taking into account, that although the ley marker buildings are consecutively placed, in reality, there will be obstructions between, nowadays especially; so, any such alignment will probably only be as 'straight' as the crow flies, or as a mapping pencil line indicates; it is unlikely that many will be gun barrel straight at ground level where walking or driving is concerned; you will invariably have to take a few detours around more recent developments such as housing estates, even the odd *landscape feature, to move along each line and find what you are looking for. *As if to confuse matters, studies suggest that the alignments aren't always entirely artificial constructs either; in some instances, they are linked with *Cathedra Botanica*... they seem to have been designed to incorporate natural features like clumps of trees, sometimes mountains, hills, rivers, streams, together with other topographic features. Maurice Chatelain, former NASA engineer claims that 'Ley Lines', when photographed from high altitude, show up quite clearly as they can be detected by 'lusher vegetation.'

I did see one such aerial photo example years ago, but I cannot find any mention of it now on the net; so, suffice to say that, I wouldn't be at all surprised that Mr Chatelain hit the bullseye with that observation.

Perhaps you could even learn to dowse for earth energies, which would certainly complete the exercise, then congratulate yourself on a job well done.

From now onwards, the once familiar will be seen in a fresh light, with entirely different eyes.

Maps, places and names will all hold a thrilling new fascination for you!

**Dowsing Via Our Own Internal Lodestone**

Perhaps most important of all – you will need a dowsing instrument or two.

It is relatively easy to 'sense' these sacral ways while manually dowsing out on site, but to electronically record the existence of Earth Energies is another matter; that is a bit trickier.

Please visit this next internet address and find how it is possible to record 'Telluric Signals'....

By far the most convenient way of gauging the strength of a particular natural energy field is usually carried out by 'Dowsing' or 'Divining' as some call it, holding either a Forked Hazel Stick, a pair of L-Shaped Swivel Rods or even a Pendulum.

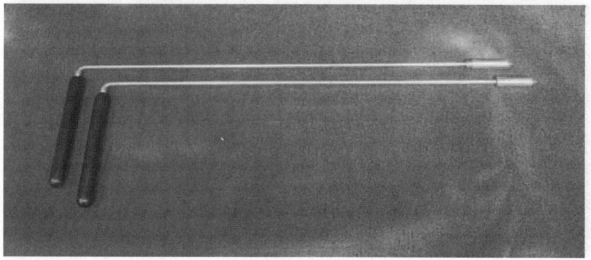

The effectiveness of dowsing can hardly be disputed.

To prove the point, did you know that every oil company in the U.S. and nigh on every commercial water company worldwide has a dowser on their payrolls?

Until recently, few people could ever have claimed to hold a definitive and provable medical or scientific explanation for the phenomena of dowsing.

No one could answer the age-old question, what causes the movement reaction in dowsing implements whenever energy is detected? where, physically unaided, L-shape dowsing rods swing outwardly/inwardly or cross themselves… or the Y-shaped hazel twig dips and rises.

Yet, here is a strong contender as to how this ancient artform works.

It is based on a unique breakthrough made by Caltech boffins.

I spotted this snippet on page three of The Los Angeles Times, (May 12, 1992) confirming that; 'Caltech scientists had discovered the presence of microscopic particles of magnetite in the brains of humans.' That is practically all they mentioned about their discovery at the time, but personally, that was an important clue for me.

Since then I've been monitoring the issue in various medical journals for years, and biomedical researchers eventually revealed this material has been detected in a variety of tissues from post-mortem human brains.

It seems that we all carry these mysterious specks; yet there is a dilemma; the brain produces its own magnetite right enough, but these endogenous nanoparticles are angular in shape, whereas they have now discovered similar brain compounds which are spherical. Their shape and other properties suggest that the spherical nanoparticles were generated during high-temperature processes like combustion… 'airborne particulate matter' that may have come from an industrial source. Thus, they are now calling this latest discovery *environmental magnetite*.

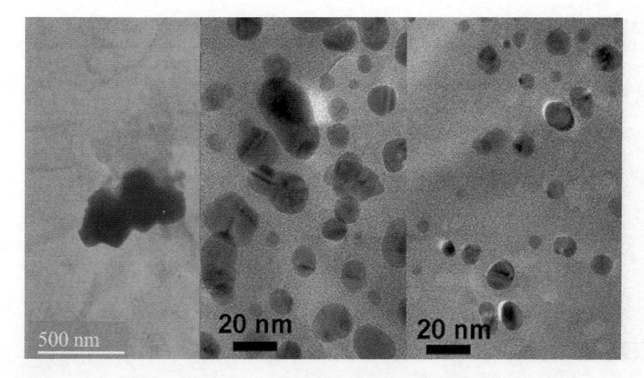

In addition to angular, biologically formed magnetite nanoparticles, (left) researchers found spherical magnetite particles in post-mortem human brains, (middle) resembling those found in polluted air (right).

**Yet, this pollution particulate invader takes nothing away from the fact there has long been evidence that some amount of magnetite forms naturally in the human brain.** Source regarding the discovery of biologically formed magnetite in brain tissue. [Kirschvink JL, Kobayashi-Kirschvink A, Woodford BJ (1992) Proc Natl Acad Sci USA 89(16):7683–7687]

# Proof of magnetic antennas in the brain

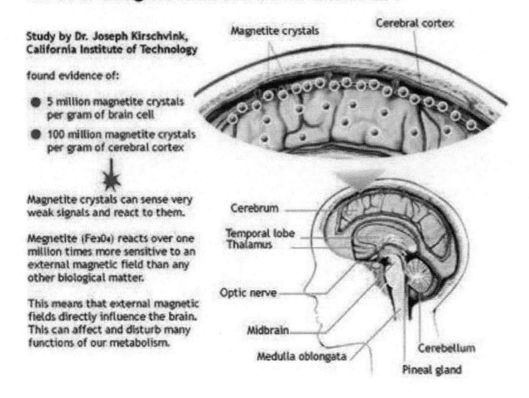

Study by Dr. Joseph Kirschvink, California Institute of Technology

found evidence of:

● 5 million magnetite crystals per gram of brain cell

● 100 million magnetite crystals per gram of cerebral cortex

Magnetite crystals can sense very weak signals and react to them.

Magnetite (Fe₃O₄) reacts over one million times more sensitive to an external magnetic field than any other biological matter.

This means that external magnetic fields directly influence the brain. This can affect and disturb many functions of our metabolism.

Labels: Magnetite crystals, Cerebral cortex, Cerebrum, Temporal lobe, Thalamus, Optic nerve, Midbrain, Medulla oblongata, Cerebellum, Pineal gland

Some are now calling these particles 'magnetic antennas of the brain'.

As I pondered what this could mean for us all, something occurred to me.

The human body itself is little more than a vertical column of water, (amounting to some 80% of its make up) and this combination of factors, (the magnetite and our watery composition) could help explain dowser's reactions.

This is my idea: When an unusual energy field, (such as the feint electrostatic charge created by an underground water spring) is happened upon in the passage of dowsing, it may cause these miniscule traces of brain magnetite to oscillate.

The result could be a transmission of explicit neural impulses to the nervous system, in turn, effecting involuntary muscular spasms to occur in the wrists – causing the dowsing implements to shift.

Same for the Y-Hazel stick.

Another name for Magnetite is **Lodestone**: lode•stone or load•stone ('loʊd•stoʊn').

Meaning... serving as a magnet; something that attracts strongly.

By the 12th century A.D., Chinese sailors were using lodestone rocks as compasses for sea navigation, and this became known as the 'guiding stone'.

**[1505–15; lode (in obsolete sense 'way, course') + stone].**

**Also, *OE* meanings of 'lode' are *lad* = 1. 'course' or 'waterway'. 2. 'an ore deposit'. 3. 'a procession'. 4. to 'go' or 'lead'. 5. to 'show the way'.**

Amazed? I know I am; let alone everything else, even now when writing this passage, recalling how we have all got nanoparticles of this lodestone, (Magnetite) in our brains... gosh, it still sends a shiver of excitement down my spine!

Another thought has just occurred to me; would the naturally occurring angular magnetite particles in our brain now be *affected by the spherical particulate foreign invaders? *Maybe even the electromagnetic radiofrequency radiation from cell phones might cause disruption to what now may be called our very own internal loadstone/magnetite GPS.

It may be wise to seek out a dedicated volume as ideas and techniques can vary from dowser-to-dowser; but personally, I found the best thing was to experiment with various methods until one finds the most successful.

But there is one aspect of earth energies which every veteran of this subject is bound to agree upon; of those which still remain active, these X-Fields are all subject to fluctuation, so their power will vary.

The causes for such vacillation may be down to crustal shift, seasonal factors together with Solar and Lunar considerations.

When walking the land in search of ancient marker site remnants, any existing flows can be further pinpointed by certain flora which show a predilection for this type of natural location.

**What's in a Name? Other Words Associated With Ley Lines**

In addition to what I have detailed so far, place names containing certain Old English Prefixes and Suffixes, (beginning or end units of pronunciation as they could be termed) might also provide advantageous links, thus increasing one's chances of making a correct assessment when researching land histories.

Examples such as 'bal', 'bel' 'bell', 'born', 'borne', 'brid', 'bride', 'burgh', 'bury'; 'coel' and 'cold', (meaning 'an omen' or a 'beacon') 'cross', 'devil', (which sometimes indicates the emphatic Christianization of a formerly Pagan area - see also 'Mary', 'Minster' and 'Temple') 'hobb', 'Jack', (which might signify a remembrance of now obsolete English fertility customs performed along the lines) 'maid', 'Mary', may', 'minster', 'stone', (boundary marker or Pagan remnant?) 'temple', 'too', 'toot', 'tot', 'twt', (which can refer to a surveillance point... *Totnes in Devon being one good example. *The steep hill at Totnes was undoubtedly once used as a surveillance point: *The name Totnes (first recorded in AD 979) comes from the Old English personal name Totta and ness or headland. Before reclamation and development, the low-lying areas around this hill were largely marsh or tidal wetland, giving the hill much more the appearance of a "ness" than today.* Ekwall, Eilert (1960)

Then there is 'well', 'witch', ''wick'... often denoting a farmstead settlement and/or a former *wiccan presence in an area. *We must not forget that the

Wiccan's, or *people of the earth* as they were referred to, practically invented farming in the Neolithic times.

In between then and now, warring, such as the Norman Conquest, resulted in the French naming of our monasteries, castles, estates etc; this, combined with poverty, pestilence and social upheaval have each caused a further transmogrification of distant folk memories.

As a result, not many place names in common use now are entirely original; having been adopted, combined with personal names, reconstructed, compounded, and palatalised.

It would be difficult to overstate the degree of loss regarding the very first titling of places.

On the positive side, old religious records can be made to work for us in a big way; often they cover the practice of lordships and acreage allotment; these often come across more like inventories than anything else, pertaining to land ownership, business and property; but even with monetary affairs featuring so prominently in the churches' estimation of a person's merit, these accounts can still be invaluable in the recovery of lost knowledge.

They are handy for instance when trying to determine whether a specific reference to 'stone' in a place name isn't just that of a humble boundary stone or even a mile marker.

It is significant to note also how plenty of other nations have their own linguistic equivalent of the word 'Ley'.

In France for instance, old denominations include 'Layon' and 'Laie' – both referring to 'pathways' of some kind; a narrow lane or passage – or 'a walk in the park, especially one lined by trees or bushes'; alternatively, one can search for terms which originate from the old French word 'alee'= meaning 'to go'.

Other countries sport names containing similar references, whose variant spellings include 'alis', 'ales' and 'alles'.

## Service to The Green Gods

There are at least 83,000 ancients sacred sites around the planet, and from everything learned, a high proportion were once used for service to the Green Gods. Mapping tests and other documentary evidence about these hallowed positions have thrown up some juicy facts.

From the middle Neolithic period onward, man began positioning a diverse array of his respected constructions in lines; these are sites, some of which directly correspond with assessed points of geodetic vigour... radiations thought to be generated through natural processes occurring within the earth.

Energies of this type have been known by various titles down the centuries... such as 'Nwyvre'... a druidical name for Gaia energies, 'Prana' and 'Vril', which is a Germanic adaptation of 'Virility'.

Surely, what we are re-discovering here is beyond 'mere fluke'; yet still, the eye-rolling denialists tell us that the propounded ley geometrics are just 'fantasy', 'psychogeography' and 'new age nonsense based on statistical coincidence'.

Even an examination by that august body The Royal Society of Statisticians, (an investigation which lasted over a decade) validated what many alternative thinkers and those with a keen appreciation of earth mysteries, had long suspected.

It was stated:

'The Incidence of aligned religious and standing stone sites across Great Britain is far greater than can be attributed to by sheer chance'; they say the facts are there – the geometry is undeniable.

Even so, we have each been taught to think in a certain way for decades, and try as some might, it is a struggle to break free from mainstream academic teachings; meaning many are suffering from truth decay! And the cure for *truth decay* is for more people to put down their phones and conduct some intensive archival research for themselves - using the prescribed methods!

Although this next observation is purely speculative, I have flirted with the idea that Ley Lines may have originally been designed to act as tracks on a circuit, through which energies flow, (or once flowed) - and certain quartz buildings may have acted as its 'components which encouraged and accumulatively stepped up/boosted the current using a sort of pre-amplification effect: Is this possible?

Could it really be that at some point in our past, the markers, (churches, stones, natural wells etc) formed a kind of framework, biologically connecting many places along these routes?

We know it was not uncommon at all for early communities to hold a faith that the planet itself could influence crop growth - thus increasing yields.

And like me, some examiners may also be aware how, up until the Ancient Monuments Protection Act was introduced, significant damage had been caused by a number of tenant farmers after hauling out 'nuisance' megalithic standing stones and carving through Neolithic/Bronze Age circles and tumuli on their land.

This happened most, shortly after the Second World War, when the 'Dig for Victory' campaign was set up by the British Ministry of Agriculture during times of harsh food rationing.

Many arrangements were removed in this manner during tree-clearance work.

Thinking about these two important points, (this ancient communal trust in Ley Lines and the fact that prehistoric sacred sites definitely once existed on farmland) a theory which crossed my mind was that the Ley Line system may have acted as an interconnected transmission network.

The idea would be for delivering earth energy nourishment from the main geomagnetic flux source lines, across longer distances via distribution lines to other areas of demand; places where those main telluric flows may have been lacking.

Just like our national electricity grid, the Ley grids might have varied in size, from covering just a few fields, to grids which covered whole counties.

A bit *out there* I agree, but that was just a feeling of mine I thought worthy of adding to the mix.

## Ocean's Dwarfed by 'Earth' Water

There are two other different networks of earth current which bear a relationship with the site alignments.

The first of these is termed the Aquiferous system – and is composed of thousands of water streams powering through subterranea.

Aquiferous ley energy is dependent on hydro-current produced by water table, (accumulated rainwater) and primary water flows.

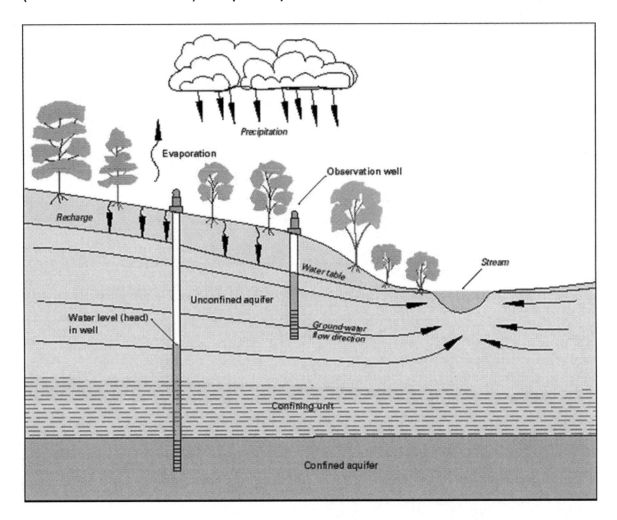

Of the two, primary, ('earth water' or 'juvenile water', as some call it) is the most interesting, as it is formed independent of rainfall; I reiterate, this has very little to do with rain!

It is the by-product of geological and chemical reactions of water trapped inside mineral seams some 400 miles below the earth's surface, in its lower mantle.

Researchers estimate that there is 5 times more water stored deep inside the earth than contained in all the world's oceans!

Under enormous pressure, 'primary water' is occasionally forced up toward earth's surface in what British dowsers call 'veins' or 'blind springs'... sometimes also known as 'domes'.

It is thrust ever upwards until hitting upon an impenetrable layer of sedimentary rock, or seam of clay, which forces the water out horizontally through fissures in the various rock strata.

Eventually these flows of mineral-rich fluid do break through to the outside world, and once established, the springs have been known to become girdled by healing claims due to their strange characteristics.

The water, when drunk, is reported to produce the feeling of a mild electric current passing through the body, and when analysed by scientists it has been reported to weigh less than ordinary water!

'Earth water' springs have popped up on or very close to ley nodal points; however, you are most unlikely to find this wonder discussed at any great length in books about hydrology - a branch of geology dealing with the study of water; and that could easily be because there are specific aspects about this particular liquid that defy an easy explanation!

To the *archaic* mind, just as droplets of rain were once thought of as *Celestial Spermatozoa* sent to fertilise the crop seed from *Father Sky*... waters directly issuing from underground courses were seen in a vaginal/clitoral/orgasmic sense.

These were viewed as the Procreative, Vascular Energies of the Great Earth Goddess; 'the milk of paradise', (to quote Coleridge) made especially fertile when stimulated by man's ritual, supplication, and procession.

Patently, as the courses of these deep waters are mainly curvilinear in pattern, it is only the systems' most vital confluence or 'aquapuncture' points, (as hardened dowsers have dubbed them) that are marked by some ley sites on the surface, possibly each tapping into the various natural currents.

Accompanying this array of hidden powers there is supposed to be one more worthwhile of mention... and perhaps, (who knows?) this may be the most crucial of all.

I am now going to reveal the existence of an Over Lighting, (above ground) influence, which is said to be far more delicate and subtler in its make-up than typical ley energies.

Early Chinese Geomancers called these flows 'Chi' – the energetic vibrational patterns found in the whole of creation, the very Life Force of Nature!

I find it fascinating how the word 'flower' is phonetically fabricated; it is comprised from FLOW-ER, indicating that the sexual textures in a plant's reproductive structures are sensitive and respondent to the over lighting flows of 'Chi'. [while I'm here think 'plant' – think 'planet'].

Dr Wolfgang Ludwig of the Institute for Biophysics, Sinzheim comments... 'we know from geo-biology about places with a special force or power, where special plants grow, which do not grow in other places.

It would be an extreme violation of the truth if we were to claim as a civilization that our scientists have explained all of nature's phenomena and wonders.'

When walking the land in search of marker site remnants, any existing, surviving geodetic or aquiferous flows, (however weak) can be further identified by certain wild flora which show a predilection for such locations.

In the countryside, pockets of meadowsweet and other wildflowers, (flow-ers) are traditionally indicative of all being healthy with nature's garden.

**The 'Spell' of Modern Language**

In a way, we have all been 'charmed' through the 'spell' of language; and it has been said more than once, that the English language is designed to trick people.

But knock it as some may... one beauty of Great Britain is that it is not yet a crime to locate and disseminate discovered secrets about our former way of life; poorly masked, linguistic tell-tale leads about a previous goddess-centred culture sometimes to be found without even stepping foot outside of your home!

Just note how today we use a whole class of curious references in everyday parlance, mottos, and sayings that we regularly employ without ever giving a second thought to the matter.

For example, such-and-such has its 'roots' in this or that, '**lay** of the land', '**mother** nature', '**mother** earth', '**mother** tongue', '**brow** of a hill', '**mouth** of a river', '**neck** of the woods', 'fountain' or 'well **head**', the slightly less hackneyed expression '**lungs** of oak', the '**branches** of a company', 'shaking like a **leaf**'; then there's 'touch **wood**', '**green** with envy', 'the **nature** of', (this, that or the other)...

And then we have '**well**'... a bit mundane to some at first glance, but like many other words it has multiple, (related) meanings, including 'good health' and 'water well' = 'to access groundwater in underground water aquifers'; this then leads to a couple of my favourites, the terms '**holy well**' and '**wishing well**', (the wish to be well?); this is particularly poignant considering how the dictionary definition for '**holy**' is '**akin to 'hale and heal', and how this in turn comes from the** *Old English/Germanic/Saxon word* '**halig = 'sacred', 'pious', 'healthy', 'whole'... but is also symbiotic of 'hole'... technically defined as in to feel 'whole', but perhaps also an alternative for 'water hole' or well?**

English is thronging with bits and pieces of other languages; it is an exotic blend of just about everything: Greek, Latin, Hebrew, Ancient Sumerian, Sanskrit etc, etc; and there are some linguistic specialists who have confirmed their suspicions to me that this cocktail has been cleverly used to conceal evidence about Man's former faith; but with a bit of back-engineering our languages can be forced to confess a great deal.

Finally, just check out the word '**belief**', (which phonetically is 'be-**leaf**')... not very exciting perhaps, but the provenance of the word 'belief' is as follows; **it is thought to have originated from the Greek word '<u>glauben</u>'; broken down, 'laub' in Greek, directly translates into 'leaf'!**

**When examined in this manner, the designation 'belief' suggests an ancient reliance on the environment in terms of Faith, Magic, Food, Materials and Herbal Medicines.**

Specific, phonetically identical words, (when used in the correct context) can also be quite revealing about the practises and preoccupations of our distant forefathers.

The word 'Divine' is a prime example; the main dictionary interpretations for this term are... 1/ 'of a god or deity'; or 2/ 'to search for water, anomalous energies or buried metals etc, using divining or dowsing implements.'

Then there is 'Temple', which is primarily defined as 1/ 'a building or place of worship dedicated to a deity or deities' or 2/ 'the region each side of the head, in front of the ear and above the cheek bone'… of course, denoting the area of our brain most commonly associated with concentration and psychic faculty.

'Pastoral' is another whose prime meanings, according to the Webster's New Collegiate Dictionary are:

> 'Of or relating to the countryside.
> or
> 'Of or relating to spiritual care or guidance of a church congregation.

Or how about the most obvious mystery word of all, (from our point of view that is)… and that word is 'Laity', (phonetically Lay-it-ee) 'lay people' = common people - as distinct from the clergy. Origin late Middle English: from lay + -ity…

And sorry, but I really can't help but hark back to those titles displaying the 'Ma'-heavy element, which are all part and parcel of a universal symbolism.

Here's another bunch; there is 'Mandala', 'Matriarch', 'Madonna', 'Magi', 'Magic', 'Maharishi', 'Mana', 'Mahatma', (an adept or sage) 'Mantra', (which, in Hinduism refers to any part of 'Vedic' literature which consists the 'Metrical Psalms of Praise)… and even the name 'Mary'… well, don't even get me started; and away from religion, (or is it?) even 'Mason', (as in Freemasonry and stonemasonry); and how about 'WoMan' and 'Man'?

For me, these words so obviously betray their linguistic origins, even though most of our dictionaries claim to have no idea where the word 'Ma' originates from; yet, it is exemplified nicely in the Celtic Earth Goddess *'Magog', venerable for 'Mother God', or that generative essence responsible for all life in the landscape.' *Gog itself is primal for 'God'; Words like 'Synagogue, (a building for Jewish religious services and instruction) originate from this very same source.

'Marriage', 'Maid' and 'Maiden' are blindingly obvious… and the reader can find many more for themselves.

More on this later.

Despite being dramatically diluted through time, vestigial traces of an original wisdom still linger and can be witnessed in the continuation of singular traditions.

Dim reflections are even to be found in our Christmas celebrations.

The Victorian adaptation of Christmas saw the bringing of small, live potted trees into one's home and the adornment of dwellings with sprigs of foliage; fair enough so far; but very few people then could have realised the rudimentary significance of such a practise.

The tree and its tub of earth possessed a twofold symbolism.

Chiefly, it equated with everlasting fertility.

The coloured bauble decorations and candles with which people would adorn their trees, portrayed the sun, moon and stars, (the cosmic canopy) under which the tree formerly lived.

One giveaway that this was a Pagan tradition through and through, could be found perched on the tree's top... the crowned fairy; this queen of all forest elementals embodies the sacred power of the feminine.

The bestowing and receiving of small tokens, and Saint Nick, (Santa... who was

originally dressed in Green –

unlike the red 'Coke' Santa we see now) a father figure for children, were the next evolutionary elaborations; then fast forward three quarters of a century or so, until we arrive at what we know of as Christmas contemporary style; complete with its annual massacre of evergreens and poultry, frenzied shopping forays and canned carol singing in the shopping malls.

Be under no illusion, this isn't me fact-weaving here; I'm not making this stuff up, no, these are what I see as actual linguistic/psychological acrobatics, cunningly used it would appear, to influence and manipulate people; the type of social engineering/mind games which have become so common that they now pervade our society from top to bottom; as commanded by those who have been running this world for a very long time.

Away from the 'Ma' syllable, we should examine the word '**Hump**', (as in earthen) '**Tump**', (dialect meaning: 1. a small rounded hill or mound; a **tumulus** or 2. a clump of trees, shrubs or grass)... which is related to '**Tum,**' (a shortening of '**Tummy**' which is informal for a person's stomach or abdomen, or the fertile earth Goddess)... and how, through word progress, much linguistic twisting and corruption, this 'Tum' syllable eventually leads us to '**Tumour,**' (an abnormal growth of tissue, whether benign or malignant)... then 'Tump' becomes associated with 'Lump'!

So sad to see such deliberate darkening and debasement of something once so cheery.

It is also sad how the word 'Cult' has even been twisted about; cult comes from the Latin word 'cultus' meaning 'care', 'cultivation', 'worship'; just consider the word Agri**cult**ure and you will see my point; it is not as the dictionary instructs us today, that 'Cult' equates with 'beliefs regarded by many people as extreme or dangerous.'

I have no wish to over-tax people with too many of these obvious and easily checkable word/name/expression fossils, but once you too eventually *crack the code* as it were, clues will be found in the unlikeliest of places using a variety of unconventional sources; and the assumption is, the only reason why these words have survived scholastic censorship, (especially during 'the inquisition years') and natural linguistic evolution, is that rather than removing them from our languages altogether, (which may have been considered a near-impossible task) they have simply been disguised.

One method of accomplishment would have been to steadily obscure any incriminating words with dual or multi definitions... an ingenious manipulation to throw us off the scent!

So, now you have seen how it works, the 'spell' of language, which has literally been spelled out; hope that the smart reader is no longer under *their* spell, (if ever they were); now it's time to get cracking!

Dozens and dozens more twists and turns could easily be explored here; out of place references spoken by countless lips; words and catchphrases that have become formulated and refined through constant usage, but which contain the memory of traditional social values from near-forgotten bygone days.

Could they be a throwback to a once wholly natural existence?

Absolutely yes... I am becoming increasingly convinced that this is indeed the case.

I see this oddball speech as a 'deep-rooted', subconscious yearning within to return to a former life of nature veneration.

One should thumb through any good comprehensive dictionary, (the older the better!) to locate the forbidden doctrine of our mother tongue, as I sometimes call it.

There, one can come across many overlooked and previously unconsidered hints, as to our ancestor's belief in earth worship and what we call Ley Lines; and when I use the term 'ancestor', actually, we don't have to go back many centuries to find clues; even as recent as the early 20th century there is evidence to suggest that many members of our wealthy aristocratic classes privately pursued the enigma of earth energies and dowsing with great enthusiasm.

**Ley Lines & Earth Energies - The Rediscovery of a Lost Wisdom**

Here's a good a motive for all the likely concealment of facts about mankind's true self.

Our hidden past of ritualised earth devotion shows up in the rosters of the British 'Church Court', who issued 'Canon Law'.

Despite the larger part of these declarations having been destroyed in the Great Fire of London, (and what was so 'great' about *that* I wonder?... as in 'great' war etc... think about it) or so they say, a residue is still to be found in Lambeth Palace and the Public Records Office at Kew.

Obviously, the fear of God alone was no deterrent to some men of the cloth, because according to surviving 'penance forms', quite a few clergymen were caught flirting with Pagan or Wiccan Craft, (witchcraft) with some publicly denouncing the Christian faith altogether upon discovery.

This resulted in priests being bought before the Church Court for trial.

A few hundred years ago, one of the most common punishments for 'the detestable sin of Paganism' by renegade clerics, was that the guilty party be forced to 'stand naked before the prosecution and whipped whilst holding a white wand, then ex-Communicated and condemned to eternal damnation'.

If, however, the priest was found guilty of the same sin in pre-Reformation times, he could just as easily have been hung at the gallows.

The Christian church eh? Such delightful people!

Stephen. E. F. Sheppard, himself a fully ordained Church of England clergyman, really dished the dirt, (so to speak) in his privately published, mammoth tome *Primeval Paganish Mnemic Activism* published in 1999, with only a limited number of copies ever printed, of which I possess one.

The result of pure dedication, Stephen's writings uncover considerable evidence about how some of the earliest Christian missionaries were left to choose their own centres and methods of operation; pious blind 'eyes' were being turned left, right and centre to earth worship and other Pagan ceremonies, which were rife in England at that time... with accusations of apostasy being levelled at quite a few church members.

I have met and talked with Stephen at length, and he totally agrees with my methodology.

He also thinks that one of the most effective weapons available to researchers of lost and suppressed knowledge, IS the study of speech processes.

'The linguistic evidence and its implications are stunning' said Stephen.

The reason why Phonology, (the study of language sound systems) is such a vital tool in our trade is simple – because people of the Middle England period tended to write and verbalise by associating letters with Oral Values.

**One of the crucial questions that Stephen asked in his book was, 'how many Christian priests in this land, both practised their Christianity, whilst continuing to hold onto their lingering and necessarily secretive, Paganistic beliefs?'**

*Funny* places them churches; and this observation by Professor George Homans of Harvard University offers ever more fuel for the fire of accusation.

This learned man who lectures on customs of the 13<sup>th</sup> century writes:

'Lammas was a feast of first fruits; it derived its name from the Anglo-Saxon *half mass* – which means 'loaf mass.'

'On that day, in the time before the Conquest, bread, which must have been made from the new wheat, was brought into the churches and blessed, and this hallowed bread was used afterwards in magic'.

From what I have read, the suggestion is strong that, whether it be inwardly when in public view, or behind locked doors, some priests were partaking of font water as symbolic milk from the earth goddess... and eating the bread as her flesh.

Christian priests drinking font water as part of their occult ceremonies?

Was this something akin to drinking 'the philosophers' wine', so often referred to in grimoires about alchemy? [Come to that, could the Biblical transformation of water into wine be an alchemical allegory?]

Is the partaking of bread and wine as the symbolic flesh and blood of Christ, itself a supplantation of a Pagan prototype?

One early church recording when translated reads: **'Whilst fearing the lord, many ministers still served their own gods 'clanculo', (in secret); this was a combination essentially resembling the attempt of many converts in that age to keep terms with both religions by attending indiscriminately, churches and the old heathen temples'.**

The overwhelming spiritual benefits that are to be had through submission to the Universal Spirit, (be that Jesus Christ, Gaia or whatever deity that one wishes to yield to at devotional sites) are perfectly documented.

**Where Does Prayer Energy Go To?**

Now, this might seem like a nonsensical question, but where *does* all the prayer energy regularly expended at places of worship up and down the country and across the world, really go to? God? If so, which God? Or does this in fact feed something else?

The prescribed manner of prayer in the Christian church is that we clasp our hands together, with our head bowed, uttering our solemn address downward...

to the ground; or in some creeds, the devoted will kneel and touch the ground with their forehead while genuflecting.

Just watch the Pope when he visits a foreign country, and the first thing that he does after getting off the plane and having walked down the steps.

Hasn't the reader ever considered this rite as a bit odd?

Ever wondered why it is that we don't look upwards as we pray, directing our communication to the sky and what we hope is the supreme deity? after all, 'he's' supposed to be 'up there', as it were – not down below!

For those of pre-Christian faith, this similar bowing of heads would have been in respect for the earth; what are the chances then, that our popular style of prayer is a Pagan throwback?

My archival delving has uncovered traces of a 'lost' wisdom; and this in turn seems to point to one main thing; that basically, our distant forefathers constructed places where people could get in touch with the spiritual world... using certain natural *laws of the land*.

There are clues which indicate a strong previous belief in the geometric and harmonic relationship between religious places and the earth itself; anciently, our planet was not considered as just a lump of rock, but revered as a living, thinking organism in its own right... and who is to say that our ancestors were mistaken?

Research shows that this strange belief involved not only the special placement of particular sacred buildings, but the arithmetical, geometrical shaping of the structures too.

Certain shapes such as the pyramid, have been scientifically proven to emit what has been dubbed 'morphic resonance', a vibrational frequency of form; as independent scientist Rupert Sheldrake terms it... 'the basis of memory in nature - the idea of mysterious telepathy-type interconnections between organisms and of collective memories within species'.

I think it quite feasible, that such *geometrical harmonics would have been thought at the time to have worked in co-ordination with certain tones and energies... chiefly, those generated by us and our planet; such reverberations are likely to have included those that are audible, such as prayer, bell sound, music etc, and others barely discernible or now undetectable with electronic instrumentation.

Worth checking out also...

http://www.beamsinvestigations.org/Keepers%20of%20The%20Living%20Earth.htm

*Historically, harmonic sequences have long had a certain popularity with church architects. Source Hersey, George L. Architecture and Geometry in the Age of the Baroque. pp. 11–12, 37–51.

Of course, what is a church spire but an elongated pyramid anyway? Which leads one to another question... whether the later church constructions were also sympathetically designed in accordance with an inherited esoteric wisdom, albeit secretly.

Those readers on the ball enough, might now begin to see that things here are really beginning to stack up.

**Inspirational Geometry**

Church spires seem to defy comprehension.

Why would anyone go to so much effort building an apparently unnecessary appendage like this, hundreds of feet into the air?

The sheer scale, specific order and symmetry of some spires, (in conjunction with the conscientiously chosen locations of many churches) have caused some researchers to speculate whether there was more to these layouts than pure aesthetics.

During a televised lecture, (the now late) celebrity scientist Professor Heinz Wolf, touched on the imposing geometry of pre-reformation church spires, and queried just 'what ARE these constructions all about?'

'Part of the British and continental landscape for hundreds of years, people just take these things for granted and see only what they have been told to expect.'

'But we really know very little in the way of hard data about the spires of pre-reformation churches.

'These things could be anything' said Heinz, 'perhaps even for launching our souls into heaven'.

This was obviously said tongue in cheek, but really, not a bad analogy considering the bulk and shape of these constructs, which come close to that standing on a N.A.S.A. launchpad!

Perhaps the professor should have looked to the teachings of Fulcanelli…

http://www.beamsinvestigations.org/Keepers%20of%20The%20Living%20Earth.htm

… and others of matching stature, for the answers he was seeking.

They inform us that the finest temples were designed using magical geomantic formulae, based on the age-old art of 'Gematria'.

Briefly explained, this is the principle wherein all the letters of the Greek and Hebrew alphabets have special numbers assigned to them, (unlike the English alphabet).

Gematria is working the 'absolute', 'ordinal', and 'reduced' values of those letter-numbers into architectural dimensions.

We are told that using measurements of, and distances between, the earth and sun, this formulation can then be applied to create a structure that is a connection point for Terrestrial and Solar Energies.

Such an effervescent commentary persuaded me to take a closer look at the sophisticated geometrics of church spires.

Before we even begin, I would like to clarify what the word 'Geometric' tells us.

It comprises two main parts: 'Geo', defined as 'of the earth' and 'metric' or 'Metron' which equates with measurement.

Thus 'Geometry', when translated literally, means 'to measure the earth'.

Looking at many examples of these strange structures, I found that the usual idea about steeples being shaped like a witch's hat is quite wrong.

Rather than conical, they are more in the way of Pyramidal; 3, 4, 5, 6 or more isosceles triangles which meet in a common vertex.

If one has ever climbed the spiral staircase within a steeple, then it is easy to appreciate why these erections are called spires.

It is clear, that the steeple interior is architecturally based on the Spiral, (the Tetrahedral Spiral to be precise, [think, *Tetrahedral* and *Cathedral*]) and is shaped that way, most likely, to act as a Resonance Funnel, drawing Tonal Patterns up from within the church, its bell tower, along with choral singing and supplication.

Speaking of the bell tower, the idea behind it was not just to produce pleasant sounds.

Bellringing marked a variety of events in olden times.

Not only was it used to summon parishioners to assemble in church, weddings, and that sort of thing, but also for the broadcast of secular time and as warnings of danger.

But these everyday uses are equally matched by other little-quoted bell practices, heralding from our archaic past.

For example, I have traced plenty of folkloric literature detailing the special value once placed by European farming communities on the precisely regulated ringing of hand bells in fields.

Bells were widely recognised as the most ideal and potent charms for blessing and protecting the land.

As if some sort of molecular dialogue was initiated between bell sound and the environment, their 'voices' were deemed to magnify fertility, ensured fruitfulness, while also putting destructive crop spirits to flight.

These accounts are furthered by archaeological papers covering Graeco-Roman times, where bells were closely associated with phalli in Bacchic virility rites.

After learning so much about the less documented role of these sirens in folklore, I was left in little doubt, that beyond routine, bell resonance chambers and church spires may have held a secret ritualistic intention behind their design.

When one stops to ponder over the word 'Spire', another mystery presents itself.

This title originated from the Latin 'Spira' and the Greek word 'Speira' meaning a spiral line.

More major clues:

**Clue 1:** Compare the phonetics of 'SPIRE' with 'PYR', (taken from 'Pyramid'' – the translation of which is 'light'.

Very similar phonetically, I think it will be agreed.

This could be sheer chance, but there again, it might not.

If it IS a coincidence, then it's a heck of a big one!

**Clue 2:** During my research, I was enthusiastically pointed in the direction of science writer John Mitchell; in particular, his seminal classic *The View Over Atlantis*.

Anyone going through this engaging book, will soon pick up as I did, that its title citation to Plato's legendary lost continent mainly alludes to the primordial foundations behind Ley Lines.

Because Mitchell reminds us that **'in most parts of the world, the churches of both England and Rome now literally mark this network of aligned geometry.**

**Their domination came to pass during the Middle Ages, when a drive to stamp out persistent 'unenlightened faiths', resulted in a host of Pagan monuments being demolished.'**

Invariably, these grounds were then used for the construction of state-approved *God Shops*.

Mitchell quotes a noted landscape researcher by the name of Ernst Borschmann, who writes about 'Dragon Faiths' and 'Lung Mei's', which intrinsically equate with the Chinese equivalent of Ley Lines.

**'Certain summits of the neighbouring mountains, often the main summit, are crowned with pagodas, small temples or pavilions to harmonise the forces of heaven and earth'.**

**'The thought is akin, for instance, to our conception of the outflow of a magnetic force from a pointed conductor; and the Chinese geomancer regards the forces of nature as a magnetic field'.**

Not forgetting a similar concept in Chinese philosophy, that of the 'Yin-Yang fields', a concept which suggests how seemingly opposite or contrary forces may actually be complementary.

**Clue 3:** It soon became evident that Spires incorporate the mathematical fundamental 'Phi', (the transcendental ratio which was used to great effect by the Greeks and Romans in their temple building measurements) as part of their make-up.

'Phi' has the value of 1. 61803.

Using this, one can produce the Phi **Logarithmic** Spiral...

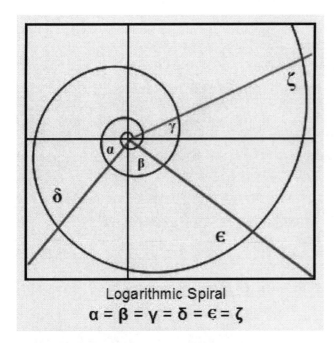

Logarithmic Spiral
$$\alpha = \beta = \gamma = \delta = \epsilon = \zeta$$

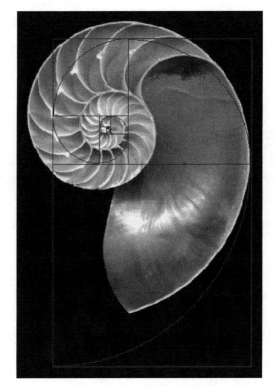

15th century spiral pillar at Rosslyn Chapel, Midlothian, Scotland: the chapel has been the subject of speculative theories concerning a connection with the Knights Templar, the Holy Grail and Freemasonry.

...a pattern which, in some abstruse way, relates to evolution!

In biology, the same Logarithmic Spiral can be found throughout nature; in mollusc shells, (such as the exquisite Nautilus) Animal Horns, the Coiled Serpent, Fir Cones, Swirling Galaxies, Gravitational Force and much more.

It is the spiral of life!

John Ivimy, mathematician and researcher of prehistory, (whose technical expertise appears throughout this section) also calls the Logarithmic Spiral the 'whirling squares'.

Phi is the limiting value of the ratio between successive numbers in something known as the 'Fibonacci Series'.

This is a series of numbers 0, 1, 1, 2, 3, 5, 8, 13, 21, 34 and 35, in which each number is the sum total of the two previous numbers.

As the numbers get progressively higher, so that ratio between each number, and the number before it, becomes ever closer to Phi.

Phi is unique in that it is the only number whose square is equal to itself plus one, and whose reciprocal is equal to itself minus one.

**Clue 4:** In the context of this investigation, the word 'Logarithm' needs closer examination.

It is seen to contain an exceedingly curious phonetic: 'Logarithm' (phonetics: Log-a - **Rhythm**; derived from 'Rhythmic' = 'Bars', 'Beats', 'Notes of a Melody'). The Rhythm of Life?

And, as many will have suspected by now, planet Earth does indeed have a sensitivity to sound.

**Clue 5:** It is usually the consensus, that most ecclesiastical buildings of the late Gothic period were conceived as a microcosm of the heavens.

Taking this factor into consideration with what we already know, wouldn't it then be logical to also expect the four basic Alchemical elements of Earth, Air, Fire and Water to be characterised in church edifices? Well, they are!

**Earth;** as exemplified by the crypt.

This hidden chamber beneath the main floor was not always used just as a repository for coffins as we tend to assume, because when the need arose, these vaults were easily transformed into Subterranean Chapels.

**Air;** as characterised by the sanctuary spire.

Apart from their functionality, spires are said to secretly honour at least three things.

Some liken the spire to an enormous Phallic Obelisk incognito… a thrusting member, surreptitiously honouring the REAL 'law of the land' - Psychosexual Energy – the spiralling reproductive force of life!

Others see the symbolism of spiritual and political power – along with man's aspiration to reach skywards.

**Fire;** as portrayed by the lighting of Altar Candles; these embody the vitalising power of the sun as symbolised by Jesus – 'the light of the world'; **verbatim; in Hebrew 'Jes' translates as 'Fire', (Sun God/Son of God?).**

**Water;** which is represented by the church font and possibly subterranean water sources; as in many cases, the water used for the Sacrament of Baptism was required to be flowing water… spring or river water. In fact, during my exploration of early churches, I have personally discovered evidence in some establishments, where the font had once been directly fed by a natural spring.

Traditionally, the term *holy water* was/is commonly employed to refer to water revered either in a Christian or Pagan context; this can originate from any water source of limited size, (including pools, streams, brooks, natural springs and seeps) which has some significance in the traditional stories of the area where it is located, whether in the form of a particular name or associated folklore, giving the attribution of healing qualities to the water.

Worth noting also, is how underground water capillaries, often being squeezed through rock strata, can generate small amounts of piezo electrical current.

Away from churches for the moment, (but maybe not *so* far away as one might think) there is yet another highly demonstrable factor which binds all these interesting info-ingredients together.

## Ground Radio

Yes indeed, there is so much more to the earth than we are generally 'sold'.

For instance: How many readers are aware that the earth actually resonates at its own frequency, (or radio band) of VLF, (Very Low Frequency) 1 kHz to 100 kHz?

more here...

https://borderlandsciences.org/journal/vol/53/n01/Vassilatos_on_Ground_Radio.html

A little-known piece of evidence comes by way of the British army, who it transpires, covertly used Earth Conduction, (currents) for Signalling purposes before and during World War 1.

Without getting overly technical - this is where pulse waveforms from a power buzzer, (better known for its application in Morse Code) can be sent long-range through the ground, without huge masts or miles of wires.

The drawback with conventional transmission antennas in the battlefield had always been enemy eavesdropping; that is why ground radio was such an advantageous method for sending important orders secretly.

Early military experiments with Earth Current Signalling entailed the burying of two electrodes into the ground a hundred meters or so apart, each connected to the antenna output terminals of a transmitter... with two more ground electrodes, (similarly spaced apart) attached to the receiving end. (radio or buzzer).

**Using this 'conduction' method, signals could be detected up to seven miles away!**

WW1 battlefield usage employed an ELF, Extremely Low Frequency transmitter, (linked from its output connections to 2x rifle bayonets, which in turn were pushed into the soil) with a matching receiver set up some miles distant, (again with absolutely no connecting wires in between) a strong signal was injected into the ground, and a weak, but identical signal, was extracted by the receiver.

Soil was found to be quite a good conductor, and ECS worked well in field situations - until that was, the introduction of domestic electricity, when current leaking from power lines began to seriously interfere with this process.

One or two of you studying this narrative may say - so what? why mention 'Radio'?

What the Dickens are you getting at here?

My point is to ask, isn't it possible that together with the natural conduction of Earth Energies, Vascular Streams plus the Psychic Expenditure from prayer at alignments of pilgrimage sites, (and even this through the ground transmission phenomenon) that 'Leys' had a very real function?

Namely, they may have served a religious purpose, however seemingly naive; maybe an attempt to connect with 'God'… a god, or gods; which, over several millennia, would have ranged from the living earth, gods of the cosmos, and latterly the traditional Christian type 'God'.

There is a possibility that the audio conduction capacity of our planet was used for sound channelling rites… earth liturgy!

I was led to this idea after I learned of a Celtic ritual that comprised Communion with Mother Earth through the use of Sound.

*Non nobis Domine, non nobis, sed Nomini tuo da gloriam… for rhythm is one of the fundamental laws of healthy soil*; as can still be witnessed by the world's so-called 'primitive' peoples, who continue to be preoccupied with the earth goddess; they, who have sung and chanted during their field labour since time in memorial!

Further ideas about the importance of sound in soil fertility reside throughout Greek classical text.

Here, the stone markers of sacred sites are consistently termed 'OMPHALI', with the 'Om' syllable in this designation sharing the same title as the famous 'OM' or 'Aum Miraat' – a primordial and highly sonorous vibration mantra used in numerous Eastern religions.

Fundamentally, what we are possibly looking at here with the ley markers, are both natural and artificial structures that were intended/designed for the purpose of working with harmonics/prayer expenditure and/or geo magnetic... and/or sound waves.

And, relating to earth's sound conduction properties, there is the trope of Natives and trackers listening to the ground to presumably hear far away animals moving - or even the distant sound of tribal drums.

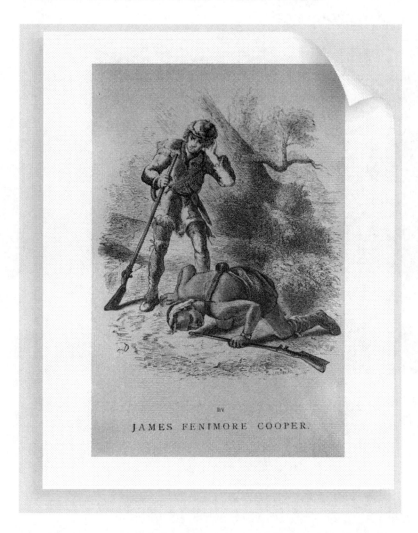

JAMES FENIMORE COOPER.

Adept trackers... Native Americans used to put their ears to the ground to hear the horses' hoofs of enemies approaching from miles away; in other countries jungle natives used the same technique of tracking.

The idea isn't as outrageous as it appears...

From the physics point of view, it has been proven that sound carries through the ground extremely well; way-better in fact, than through the air.

All the indications are, the very structure of Earth Organism Gaia is a great conductor of sound; but even more interesting is the idea that 'she' could be able to absorb many audio pitches, (such as the devotional tones generated by supplication) and Biosynthesise these into her Life Pulse.

A conclusion of fact? No, not 100%, although 'resonance' is certainly high up on my suggestion list.

According to Jimmy Goddard, author of *The Hidden Unity*, the supporting columns of The Templar Foundation in London City, (a church financially sponsored by the legal profession and built by the Knights Templar as their English headquarters) can be made to produce a Middle 'C' note by choral singing.

This detailing may ultimately prove to be of great import, because I have read of other authorities also citing 'Middle C' along with 'F' and 'G', (a range beginning at some 256 cycles per second) as 'the natural keys of life'.

None of this comes as any surprise to me; because when marvelling over their intricate architectural design and amazing auditory properties, it has often crossed my mind that these buildings could have been purposely built as finely tuned instruments!

Acoustically-speaking, just as the insides of a violin reveal a miniaturized equivalent of a music hall... church buildings seem to have also been designed in a similar fashion, with sound generation in mind.

In all probability, harmony is not only limited to sound.

Two things may be in harmony with each other, such as when the topographical co-ordinates of a place location and the architectural geometrics of a building have a solid mathematical relationship, involving whole numbers and natural constants like Pi, (the radius of a circle/circumference) or Phi, (the Golden Mean).

According to common scientific models, the magnetic field of Earth is also composed out of resonances, radiating out in lines with two different qualities.

These are South and North resonances.

'Demiurge' is the title awarded to the skill of impelling earth to yield its forces through dance and prayer, as detailed in 'Timaeus', a unique digest written by the Greek Philosopher Plato.

In one part of his esoteric teachings he talks about 'Demiurge' as the control of *anima mundi*, (the animated 'world being') and describes planet earth as 'the fairest and most perfect of intelligible beings, framed like one visible animal comprehending within itself all other animals of nature'.

Top-notch researcher Tom Graves speculates how, apart from their obvious fertility connotations and phallic symbolism, the Maypole could have been physically comparable, (or at least complimentary) in its function to the megalithic standing stones.

These needles of wood, (as he calls them) might have been vibrationally activated by the elaborate motions and reverberations of their dancers.

Oddly, as they are platted, the maypoles' ribbons appear to simulate something close to the figure for DNA, the main chromosome constituent of all organisms; and this is in addition to the spiral colours

already painted on the pole!

DNA or Deoxyribonucleic Acid takes the form of a double helix spiral... the Caduceus.

First originating in ancient Syria, (what is now Iraq) the Caduceus badge also represents the genetic blueprint and has been used ever since to signify the Solstices, the cycles of nature, homeopathic powers, and at this present time it is the medical profession's main logo.

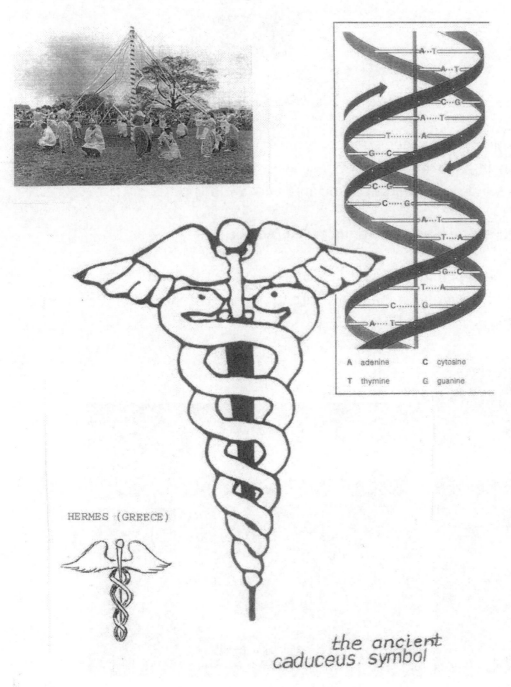

A  adenine          C  cytosine

T  thymine          G  guanine

HERMES (GREECE)

the ancient
caduceus symbol

genetic blueprint

Written works dealing with classical symbolism, say that when portrayed in this manner, one or two snakes represent the Universal Growth Spiral, and the staff symbolises the *axis mundi* around which all life revolves. [it is even wondered whether there is a similar, but hidden significance behind the $ Dollar icon, known

by its other name of the 'Wand of Power'.]

As with the old traditions of Morris Men street plays, please, if you get the chance, watch their dancing and other performances live, because there you will see the survival of ancient agricultural rites associated with various cults.

Now, please ruminate over the Harvest offering called the Corn Dolly.

Is there a special meaning behind its basic design, which despite the addition of some novelty shapes, has always been manufactured to the same traditional platted, spiral cage pattern?

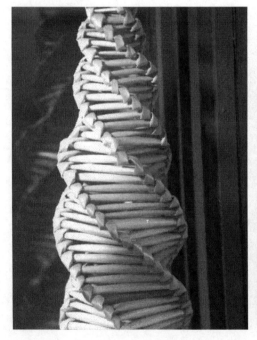

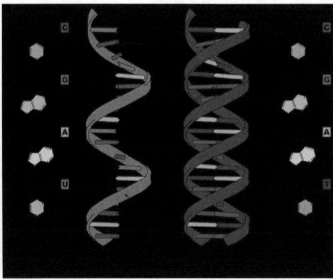

The 'Corn Dolly' – a harvest trophy          DNA

Despite obviously lacking the scientific and technological fineries of today, could it be that our Shamanic Forefathers possessed an elementary, backwoods appreciation about the existence of DNA?

Whether it was sexual or scientific, either way each of these philosophies had an identical end goal.

Everyone involved was trying their utmost to ensure that the planet would yield good harvests and give protection to their livestock.

From all I have studied, even in the farm fields, no opportunity was ever lost to stimulate Gaia's energies.

Back to our Maypole again... and a quick fact-burst here before I continue: Virtually every village and town once boasted its own maypole.

In London for instance, the Strand saw a 134ft high pole erected during the time of Elizabeth 1, on a spot now occupied by the church St Mary-le-Strand; the pole was destroyed by the Puritans in 1644.

Another similar London landmark was situated in Cornhill, where a great Maypole or 'shaft' was set up outside the church of St. Andrew.

The dancing of people under the pole throughout the month of May, gave the church its present name of St. Andrew Undershaft.

Other writings tally with Graves' observation.

Country folk of those times it seems were not, (like the old saying goes) as green as they were cabbage looking.

These people were possessors of an inherent wisdom centred on nature; possibly able to summon and utilise two types of subterranean current through implements like the megalith and latterly the Maypole.

A knack presently lost to the man on the street, urging the earth to yield with staves and poles was actually a recognised agricultural routine... with kindred customs which can be traced back as far as 8,000 BC to a Sumerian group known as the 'Annanage'.

And if that wasn't enough, the gravity of this next revelation should hit the astute learner right between the eyes.

Several leaders of folk art have described how the very old intention behind the Maypole and its ribbons, was that each would be a pilot for its dancers to follow: same with the stone circles.

In an almost hysterical state, participants would trace a repetitive, lively pattern in order to 'wind-up' or 'encourage' the latent ground energies to rise for promotion of crop growth, human fertility and healing purposes.

This wiccan 'seasons' rhyme reminds us a bit about the old ways:

*We dig and we plough, and we hoe and we sow,*

*It's best done in moonlight, as you ought to know,*

*We pray to the Goddess to make the seed grow.*

*Singing too rali, oo rali, oo rali o.*


*We fill up her furrows, the seeds lie below,*

*With patience we waite though they germinate slow,*

*Then all of a sudden, the seeds start to grow;*

*Singing too rali, oo rali, oo rali o.*


*The sun shines upon them, they're all doing fine,*

*The crops in the fields are growing in line,*

*They shoot through the earth and they all start to show.*

*Singing too rali, oo rali, oo rali o.*

*We get on our broomsticks and dance around the fields,*

*this causes the meadows to give up their yields.*

*The higher we jump and the higher they grow.*

*Singing too rali, oo rali, oo rali o'.*


*And then comes the harvest when all things are ripe.*

*We honour the goddess with song, drum and pipe,*

*And gather the crop before we get snow.*

*Singing too rali, oo rali, oo rali o.*


*So, praise be the Goddess who makes all things thrive,*

*And give us the fodder by which we survive,*

*We give adoration before she must go.*

*Singing too rali, oo rali, oo rali o.*

Shared unconscious remembrances about the energy aspect of these rituals, are again insinuated in the work 'Music and the Soil', published in 1908.

This compelling piece of Edwardian documentation that relates to analogous folk traditions, speaks about the Plough Stots, a sword dance first belonging to Whitby Moors.

'The village tailor made us black knee breaches. The girls who came to our dancing and singing parties sewed our baldricks and ribbons. We were about fourteen men in all'.

'We worked hard at the figures, but above all we concentrated on the rhythmic intensity and flow of this dance.

'The basis of the dance is the circuit of energy whose current passes from man to man through the linking swords. We made a conscious endeavour to stimulate this current, concentrating our minds and senses so that the tension should at no point be broken.

'We also concentrated on that peculiar sword dance step, a lilting fall from the ball of the foot to the heel in which the feet become like magnets drawing from and caressing the ground in rhythmic pulses'.

The application of emotional and physical energy through Song, Dancing and Prayer, (harmonics) played an important role in encouraging the ebb and flow of biological and geological forces deemed to be present in the land.

In 'Looking for the Lost Gods of England' it is detailed… 'the activation of the Mother Earth' was achieved through 'recitation of power-inducing invocatory prayer; there takes place the 'anointing of the fertilising organ' to make it 'potent with semen'.

Again, this is detailing the sexual, emotional, and psychic expenditure from British native ritual.

These matters were further covered by K. Herbert; her excellent book also talks about priestly connivance in the events.

Janet and Colin Bord, the writer/archivist team responsible for dozens of folklore volumes writes: 'Between the sowing of the seed and the harvesting of the crop, the whole community, who all depended on a successful harvest, performed many rituals to encourage the crops to grow.

One of the most widespread in former ages, but not so today, was the ceremonial coupling of male and female in the fields at Springtime.

'This has been interpreted by all authorities as imitative magic, or 'laying the fields open to the workings of fertility'.

'We suggest an alternative interpretation, that by experience it was known and accepted that the energy emitted by the participants in the act of sexual union would supplement and encourage the flow of natural energy inherent in the land, and thereby promote crop growth.

'One couple would have a small effect; many couples would have a much greater effect. Mircea Eliade states that 'as many couples as possible' used to mate in the fields at this time'.

Ostensibly, the church later hijacked our love affair with the land and matters were swiftly sanitised.

The Pagan community were to see such rituals re-packaged as 'Rogation' or 'Rogationtide'. The word rogation comes from the Latin verb 'Rogare', meaning 'to ask'; this was observed with processions and the Litany of the Saints, April 25, the Monday, Tuesday and Wednesday before Ascension Day.

The Ancient Custom of Blessing the Fields on Rogation Sunday at Hever, Kent Taken February 1967

The faithful typically observed Rogation days by fasting and abstinence in preparation to celebrate the Ascension, and farmers often had their crops blessed by a priest at this time.

Wikipedia tells us that the Rogation Day ceremonies are thought to have arrived in the British Isles some time during the 7th century.

The oldest known Sarum text regarding Rogation Days is dated from around 1173 to 1220.  Celebrations in southern England are described, in which processions were led by members of the congregation carrying banners representing various biblical characters. At the head of the procession was the dragon, signifying Pontius Pilate, which would be followed by a lion, signifying Christ. After this there would be images of saints carried by the rest of the congregation. Many torches were present at each procession, weighing between 42 lb (19 kg) and 27 lbs (12 kg), which were bought by the church and parishioners jointly.'

Sarum texts from the 13th and 15th centuries show that the dragon was eventually moved to the rear of the procession on the vigil of the Ascension, with the lion taking its place at the front. Illustrations of the procession from the early 16th century show that the arrangements had been changed yet again, this time also showing bearers of reliquaries and incense.

During the reign of King Henry VIII, Rogation processions were used as a way to assist crop yields, with a notable number of the celebrations taking place in 1543 when there were prolonged rains. Even before religious sensibilities turned towards the puritanical, there were concerns about the lack of piety at such events.

There is a suggestion that 'Rogation' is a Christian play on the title 'Rotation'... as in dance movement or the rotation of soil thereof.

Not convinced about the corruption of Rogation? First think of the linear, wavy patterns, peaks, and troughs of a ploughed field; then think of the phonetic similarity between Rogation and our modern term Corrugation, [Definition of **corrugation**. 1 : the act of **corrugating**. 2 : a ridge or groove of a surface that has been corrugated. Example - **Corrugated**... as in roof cladding - corrugated steel sheets etc.

To some extent, the modern English language that is taught in schools today is either a corruption, or the product of some carefully crafted social engineering!

Think also, of the Precise definitions of Ascension: *Theological* meaning 'The passing of Christ from Earth into heaven'. Vintage *Dictionary* definition 'To go or move upward – to grow' and 'To make humble, request or to plead'.

Could it even be, that participants of today's church rites are merely *going through the motions*, completely blind to the more earnest intention behind all mainstream religious celebration?

Speaking of which, it might be recalled by some older generations, that up until just a few years ago the church also observed the tradition of 'Plough Monday', on the first Monday after January 6; and on the Sunday after this came the 'Blessing of the Plough' ceremony; whatever happened to these customs?

During the Pagan epoch, (and even today in some parts) most countries had their own equivalent of Ground Energy Winding.

Close relatives are dances performed by the American-Indian Rain Man; the Cahokia Aztecs, (chicane and spiral dances); rituals vis-à-vis the Aboriginal 'Song Lines' of Australia; the Whirling Dervish dances; the 'Z-Ceremony' that used to be conducted around The Great Pyramid of Egypt, and the repetitive path that pilgrims would walk within a Maze or Labyrinth, again, once a common spectacle.

The spiritual Shaman would have considered these places of devotion as Energy Receptors, (Tachyon?) or 'cells' in Gaia's bio-nervous system; with each being an axis point to conduct harmonic impulses of earth energy... spiralled upwards by the dancers' rhythmic motions.

Rhythm is the fundamental law of a healthy planet.

**Ever Wondered About the Effects of Psychic Expenditure?**

After conducting thousands of laboratory-controlled experiments over a 10-year period, Professor Robert Jahn of Princeton University, arrived at a conclusion that truly put the cat among the academic pigeons; and maybe that's why his work virtually disappeared without a trace.

He stated that 'praying, hoping and wishing can have an effect on the physical world.'

With sheer mind power, or PK, (Psycho Kinesis) his group of experimenters were successfully able to influence computer programmes used to generate random patterns and pictures.

In a report featured in *The Paranormal, Beyond Sensory Science*, (Arkana Books) Dr Percy Seymour, outspoken scientist from Plymouth University claimed that the phenomenon of PK is caused by 'streams of highly charged subatomic particles'.

He says – 'intense feelings can leave Electrical Tracks in their wake'.

It has even been demonstrated that thought-energy possesses a certain polarity!

Then there were the through the ground experiments performed by famous inventor Nikola Tesla, the man with a dream of worldwide wireless transmission of electricity, which proved highly successful... Google it!

When active, the ley grid has attracted all kinds of paranormal activity along its roads, churches, stumps, tumps, humps and bumps; sighting reports have ranged from Ectoplasmic-type Mists, floating Orbs to silhouettes and decidedly human and strange animal facades.

And, not only *along* these ways, but above them also, aerially; where even myself and my partner have been privileged to observe some curious events, (let us call them 'astronomical')... one of which reminded us of a giant green tadpole complete with undulating tail... 'swimming' through the air!

Whether these things are the result of mystical, electrical or magnetic properties, or a blend of all, it can only be guessed at; but let me put it this way, at times, in some of my research logs, I have taken to using the title of 'Prayer Lines' rather than 'Ley Lines'... and I will tell you why in a moment.

It might be that you only spot these 'Phantasms' out of the corner of your eye.

Many tend to be just misty outlines, but by all accounts, a few can be exceedingly realistic, complete apparitions, solid-looking.

When fortunate enough to witness the latter face-to-face as it were, (of course, certain types do not even have *faces*, simply a black void where a 'face' should be) then, more than likely, they will perform a vanishing act!

Like movie recordings in the ether, occasionally triggered and replayed by some unknown factor, I sometimes wonder, just why is it that presences of this kind are attracted to the ley grid at all?

Where do they even originate from? Some sub-astral plane from a neighbouring dimension?

Good or bad, such phenomena may make themselves known in a variety of ways; from effecting noises, flashes, the sensation of touching a witness/witnesses or simply emitting an odour like a cheap perfume or cigarette smoke; made I think, simply to alert one to their presence.

Years ago, I witnessed a manifestation of this type myself; it's incredible to see as they travel/drift along in a steady, determined fashion; a bit like someone or some-thing on a mission... is my best description.

I've often deliberated whether these phenomena are related to 'earth bound'/lost souls/trapped spirits.

My reasoning for now and then switching to the title 'Prayer Lines', is a suspicion that I have concerning the phantom-forms preferred haunt... namely near to sites of devotion.

I have wondered, by these things moving over the lines, (which will inevitably bring them to a place of worship on-route) are they in fact seeking human help? Is it their attempt at finding salvation... their wish to 'pass-over' properly... 'into the light', (to coin a phrase)... to the 'other side'?

I have also pondered over another possibility... that the lines, (rather like a Scalextric track) are powering individual phenomena... or perhaps 'they' feed off it.

**Don't walk so close to me!**

Farnham is said to be the most haunted town in Surrey, and one day back in the Spring of 2004, it certainly lived up to its reputation!

A true and accurate report of a probable ghost encounter in Farnham, Surrey, UK

The reason that the two of us singled out Farnham for a visit, is because its parish church is a significant ley landmark on the Pilgrim's Way, the ancient route from Winchester to Canterbury, something we are most interested in; parts of this building actually date back to the middle ages and it stands on foundations of a 7th-century Saxon church!

We headed towards St Andrew's via the West entrance, along a very old flagged pathway flanked by aged buildings: Apart from its lovely Gothic revival stained glass window, we found the interior of the church itself quite standard and a bit boring to be honest; so we left and went to have a look around to see if we could perhaps spot any unusual architectural carvings outside; the two of us walked in an anti-clockwise direction along the pathway as we continued our exploration.

Where the track splits and meets the path coming in from Downing Street, we were suddenly joined by a very strange young woman who seemed to appear from nowhere and began walking directly behind us; so close, that if we had suddenly stopped there would definitely have been a collision!

We were both thinking how incredibly rude she was.

People were sitting on benches in the grounds, and some politely looked up as if to say 'good day' as we passed them, but we noticed they were not acknowledging the girl, only us.

We furtively glanced over our shoulders several times and became rather concerned; not only because of her uncomfortably close proximity to us, but each time we looked, we saw that she was wringing her hands all the while; the girl was obviously distressed about something and we could even hear her breathing rapidly.

Just our luck I thought, to have a mad woman on our tails.

From what we could make out, she was dressed in something like a 1970's overcoat which had a fitted waist.

We continued on the upper path round the Church, hoping to get back out onto West Street and perhaps shake off this girl following right behind us; the situation was getting rather silly, so we stopped, (half expecting her to clip our heels when we did so) as we had whispered between ourselves that we were going to confront this person and ask her to either pass by, or at least desist from walking so close to us; but to our shock and amazement, when we turned around we saw that she had vanished!

Next, we quickly ran back to the Church grounds and checked everywhere, but the girl was not to be seen.

Later, we conducted some internet research hoping to find out whether anyone else had ever reported a similar experience for these parts, but couldn't find anything that exactly matched; however, we discovered the legend of how, back in the 1970's, a young woman had climbed the tower of St Andrew's Church, Farnham and threw herself off to her death... although apparently, there is no official record of the claimed suicide.

Was this the very same girl that we had seen?

For us, our strange encounter was simply too coincidental for this NOT to be the case.

Sometimes, paranormal 'entities' show up on photos that aren't seen by the human eye at the time of shooting – unintentional captures.

Just like this next example, sent into us by one of our BEAMS members, Psychic Julie Goring.

Above: Crop of mystery image; family cat and unknown figure; photo copyright of Julie Goring

Anomalous, Spirit-Type Figure Captured in Swindon, Wiltshire, 2012 or 13

Description: 'This picture was taken some years ago, (2012 or 2013) by my daughter in her garden in Wiltshire, UK: She was photographing their family cat; the brown figure behind it is a complete mystery and only showed up on the one photo; the next shot taken straight after, same spot, didn't show anything unusual.'

Above: Cropped and brightened detail of the figures' head/face.

BEAMS analysis: As seasoned researchers we have had a good deal of experience in the analysis of unexplained imagery; and there is little doubt in our minds that the above case photo is genuine, and shows an unintentional capture of something which we cannot normally see with the naked eye; probably an incorporeal form which varies in its vibration/frequency to anything in our physical plane of existence.

Having studied so much evidence of this nature, we can verify that the countenance of such human-like figures can often appear somewhat 'alien' to our earthly eyes; perhaps distorted, deformed, out of proportion and/or even with animal-like features; we think that this particular example from the Swindon report looks a bit like a bear.

A convenient label that investigators usually put on this type of image is 'ghost', 'spirit' or 'phantom', (and we can be just as guilty of doing the same ourselves sometimes); yet that is only guesswork, as we really have no idea whether these things are anything to do with the dead: So, for reference purposes here, in this specific report, let's call the figure a 'paranormal entity'.

Unsurprisingly, these photographed entities often have a most unusual aspect about their facial features; which can be so extreme, (as with the above image) that those of a religious persuasion might even refer to them as 'demonic'; but why jump to such a conclusion? who is to say exactly how a 'demon' should look in any case?

On the flip side of the debate, the same can be said of 'angels'; maybe the Biblical artists who have for centuries portrayed angelic beings in their customary Utopian manner, with wings and/or playing a harp, have got it all wrong; maybe the figure under discussion here is in fact an angel... who can say for sure?

Just because a supernatural phenomenon fails to meet our romantic preconceptions/expectations in its ways or appearance, does not automatically mean it is something diabolical.

Using the same religious parlance, be they 'angels' or 'demons', they are surely all 'God's creations' in his 'house of many mansions', (or dimensions)... and for us here at BEAMS, they serve to further our understanding about what exists at various levels of the paranormal.

Plus, whatever you do, you must see this video:

https://www.youtube.com/watch?v=Jkpmtn1xWEw

'Ghost' Captured - Cobham Manor, Kent - The Pilgrim's Way. 1980's Footage - Verified Real.

Many open-minded students will, by this time, have joined parts of the Ley Line puzzle together; but please don't stop reading, there's more!

The picture is only partially completed... there is even evidence to suggest that Ley Lines could well play a major part in the appearance of some Unidentified Aerial Objects!

Do as I have done, and plot unidentified aerial phenomena on Ordnance Survey maps for many years, and you will soon begin to see what we are dealing with here.

**UFOs**

Finally, after years of re-discovering lost alignments and marking them onto map sheets, it became noticeable to me that UFOs often occur over Ley Line areas... areas that have lines of early marker-buildings and various other sites of worship to their credit; exhaustive cross-checking between my maps and the BEAMS Reports database, confirmed this conclusively.

Filmed and reported UFO activity above these lines certainly suggests to me some kind of relationship between the leys, and strange aerial objects.

Agreed, a percentage of the UFOs seen and recorded over these places may well be earth-generated luminosities; airborne masses of highly-charged energy plasma which are somehow triggered by the aforementioned subterranean forces; these are often classed as 'earth light' phenomena.

Yet there is a sticking point here, as many of the mysterious aerial objects that I have had the opportunity to study, appear to display controlled/sentient characteristics; and it goes without saying really, that if this same type of phenomena had been witnessed by our distant ancestors, those onlookers would have doubtless viewed the UFOs as Spirits or 'Gods' - and perhaps built their sacred henge sites etc accordingly, to where such miracles in the sky occurred; as above, so below?

The unequivocally manipulative film The Wizard of Oz, 1939, complete with its green-faced 'wicked witch', 'talking trees' and the (*pay no attention to that man behind the curtain*) Wizard himself, may be pertinent to our study.

Any buff of 'earthlight' UFOs would have been fascinated by this movie, as there is a scene where the 'good' witch Linda floated down to Dorothy while housed inside an incandescent bubble, (the classic *Amber Gambler* luminous event as they are sometimes referred to) no less an 'Identified Flying Object' of the earthlight kind; a very clever use of imagery.

The inspiration behind this MGM epic was a book written in 1900; its author was Frank Baum, high ranking member of the infamous occult group The Theosophical Society, run by Russian emigre Madame Helena Blavatsky.

The occultist writer of this story admitted that initially he used 'OZ' as a clever coded nickname for the Ancient Egyptian god 'OSIRIS'!

And here is another connected twist; how many people are aware, before becoming saddled with such sombre titles as 'Lord of the Underworld', 'Lord of the Dead', 'Lord of Darkness' and similar handles, the Green God Osiris was first revered as an overseer of Vegetation and Fertility!

Based on my own studies and experiences, here are what I suggest that many of the finest reported UFO sightings might include:

Earthlight UAP - Unidentified, Natural Earth & Aerial Phenomena, (still, largely unexplained).

Proto entities - (primitive aerial lifeforms; giant, but short-lived amoeboid-type creatures).

Multidimensional or trans-dimensional forms/apparitions/'visitors'.

Off-planet objects – craft and intelligences.

I suspect that many UFOs are produced by the unification in earth's atmosphere, of solar magnetic forces, working in league with favourable geo-magnetic energies emanating from the planet's core.

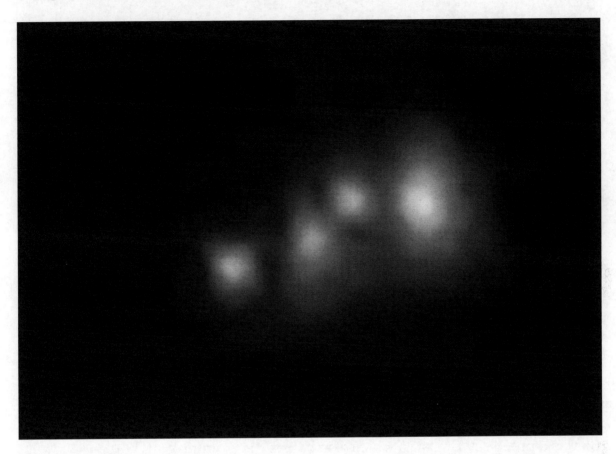

Unusual object/objects captured by the author over a Ley in Farnborough Hants, UK, 07/09/15

Video here...

https://www.youtube.com/watch?v=prJq9twkC8o

Worth noting also, is how, (from a Ley Line perspective) where we live, the historic Farnborough Convent and Abbey, (grounds which contain a secret 'mini Stonehenge' of ancient sarsen stones, already linked in a previous section of this book) are both visibly in our line of sight.

http://www.beamsinvestigations.org/FARNBOROUGH%20-%20A%20Mini%20Stonehenge1.html

Here is another example from Farnborough.

Photo of the Hog's Back area and artists impression insert

It was Easter, Saturday, 6th April 2007 when we had our most dramatic Close Encounter experience with a UFO so far.

Our friend Jonathon was visiting us in Farnborough for a long weekend.

During the evening, we all got in the car to go up on the Hogs Back A31, with the intention of conducting a small sky watch there; we arrived at about 8:45pm.

The Hog's Back is a noted Ley Line area which also boasts the Pilgrims Way crossing on its Southern side, running from Farnham, which is a good reason why this location is favoured by us for sky watching purposes.

Jonathon, who is a fellow mysteries researcher, had never been to this spot previously, but for me and Hil, this has become a good place to indulge in our passion, (no, not that!) of searching the heavens for possible UFOs - Unidentified Flying Objects.

We parked up as we normally do, wound the windows down, and along with our extra passenger, we began our vigil of the sky, gazing in the direction over Guildford, Surrey.

I remember me looking up and saying, (jokingly) 'please give us a good sighting, nothing like last time, something so small that my camera would hardly pick it up, thank you!'...

...a sarcastic reference to a previous watch that we did which was a complete waste of time, where all we had seen were tiny LITS, (Lights in the sky) pinpricks that could have been anything.

It was a night of good visibility, clear with a bit of high cloud; the three of us sat quietly, binoculars and camera at the ready; we had been there a while, and I think that we were becoming slightly resigned to the idea that, (as with about 95% of the time when sky watching) we were not going to see anything out of the ordinary that evening.

But, just how wrong could anyone be?

Suddenly in the distance, something caught our attention; our jaws dropped!

Through the cloud appeared the most beautiful, red/purple mass of light, roughly oval in shape, which was steady, no flashing, with dazzling rays of brilliance emitting from it.

To our naked eyes this thing was huge, far bigger, and brighter than any aircraft lights, and of a most unusual colour, the likes of which we have since failed to see or match. (Only through mixing the paints in an artist palette, have we come close.)

We all got out of the car, with me videoing and Hilary studying the situation through high-powered binoculars; she informed us that there were definitely 'no wings, tail or navigation lights' in fact, there was no metallic structure at all that she could make out, just this brightly illuminated oval.

What we were watching was obviously under intelligent control, as 'the mass' began to gently descend in a perfectly straight manner, over in the near distance and down behind some trees...

None of us could detect any sound, which one would expect for an object so big.

It was covering a large area between Stoughton/Jacobs Well near Guildford, so we began calculating the size of this oddity.

Using Guildford Cathedral on the horizon as a reference point, we estimated that the UFO was at least half the size of the building!

So transfixed were we by this aerial spectacle, we had even become oblivious to the usual noise of traffic swishing by.

This 'thing' was still as brightly illuminated as it descended, exactly as we had first seen the object at higher altitude; then our view as to exactly where it landed, (if indeed, it did land at all!) became obscured by trees.

I tried videoing as much of the UFOs' movements as I could.

After this the object was gone; we all gasped and started saying things like 'wow, that has got to be in the papers tomorrow', and 'we are never going to see anything like that again in our entire lives'...

But later, at 9:15 pm, either the same or a similar object, once again suddenly appeared through the cloud cover, exactly as it had done before, this time though our guest Jonathon excitedly said to me, 'have you got a torch in the car?', 'yes' I replied – 'quick, shine it at the object' Jon said...

Normally I wouldn't dream of doing such a thing as it could prove dangerous to conventional air traffic; but egged-on by Jon's urgings, I grabbed my high candlepower halogen spotlight that I always carry in the boot in case of breakdowns, and flashed its powerful beam at the UFO, hoping to reveal any possible body/structure that might be behind all its radiance.

I swear, that the second my torch beam shone into the sky, the UFO instantly vanished before our eyes there and then!

This sudden vanishing left me feeling slightly guilty, as if I had offended whoever or whatever was responsible for the UFOs appearance by shining the torch beam on them; maybe 'they' saw this light as a threat and acted protectively in response.

I thought that I had frightened them away! but we waited to see if anything else would happen, and incredibly it did!

At about 9:30pm something suddenly came through the clouds over the same area... it was our UFO yet again!

As with the first object all of us had seen, no torches this time, instead we just watched the object in all its beauty and gracefulness, feeling privileged as we did so.

We waited half an hour longer, but that was it: We left the lay-by feeling elated after having experienced 3 incredible sightings all in one night!

Now for the bad news: Unfortunately back then, all we possessed was a really early, basic camcorder... a *dinosaur* that was fine when shooting in the daytime, yet which struggled to record in the dark as it had no 'night shot' or anything that *fancy*; even so, I had taken the gamble and attempted to video the UFO, but on replay, there was little of what we had witnessed, much to our disappointment, but not to my surprise.

Damn it! I muttered when I played the tape back; just blackness and fuzz, that's practically all there was; hardly anything had been recorded except static and a couple of feint frames that showed a giant, glowing red orb, which is not how we saw the object at all.

What we had seen was best described as a pink-red chandelier of light.

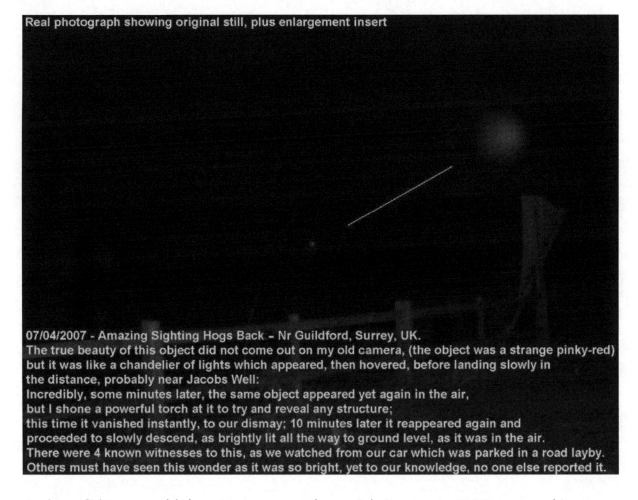

Real photograph showing original still, plus enlargement insert

07/04/2007 - Amazing Sighting Hogs Back – Nr Guildford, Surrey, UK.
The true beauty of this object did not come out on my old camera, (the object was a strange pinky-red)
but it was like a chandelier of lights which appeared, then hovered, before landing slowly in
the distance, probably near Jacobs Well:
Incredibly, some minutes later, the same object appeared yet again in the air,
but I shone a powerful torch at it to try and reveal any structure;
this time it vanished instantly, to our dismay; 10 minutes later it reappeared again and
proceeded to slowly descend, as brightly lit all the way to ground level, as it was in the air.
There were 4 known witnesses to this, as we watched from our car which was parked in a road layby.
Others must have seen this wonder as it was so bright, yet to our knowledge, no one else reported it.

And, as if things couldn't get any worse, these sightings were NOT reported in any of the local or national papers.

It was as if no one else had seen any of this, which we find very hard to believe, as it all happened so close to a busy dual carriageway!

We strongly suspected a cover up!

Hilary is ex-MoD and a trained observer: As for myself, I have had over 20 years of experience in the field of UFO research, and we can honestly say that what we encountered that evening was something very strange, the likes of which we were totally unfamiliar with: We had never witnessed anything like it before, nor have we observed anything like it since.

It wasn't atmospheric phenomena, it wasn't an airship, a hot air balloon, Chinese lanterns, flares nor any sort of conventional aircraft, (as some cynics have tried to suggest) but a legitimate, intelligently controlled UFO.

Our Hogs Back observation was remarkably similar in certain respects, to another sighting report that we have since discovered, made by someone else in this area, back in 1977.

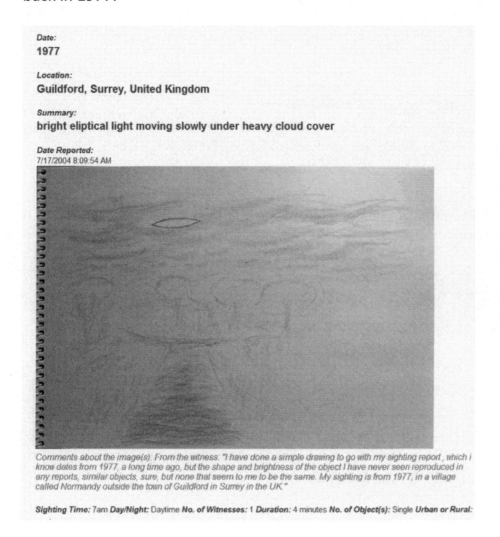

Date:
1977

Location:
Guildford, Surrey, United Kingdom

Summary:
bright eliptical light moving slowly under heavy cloud cover

Date Reported:
7/17/2004 8:09:54 AM

Comments about the image(s): From the witness: "I have done a simple drawing to go with my sighting report, which I know dates from 1977, a long time ago, but the shape and brightness of the object I have never seen reproduced in any reports, similar objects, sure, but none that seem to me to be the same. My sighting is from 1977, in a village called Normandy outside the town of Guildford in Surrey in the UK."

Sighting Time: 7am Day/Night: Daytime No. of Witnesses: 1 Duration: 4 minutes No. of Object(s): Single Urban or Rural:

+ 2 more genuine, classic examples of a saucer-shaped UFO seen at close range, on, or flying over The Hogs Back.

Please see here...

http://www.beamsinvestigations.org/1983.html

to read the close encounter case of 77 year old, Alfred Burtoo of Aldershot, Hampshire UK...

and here...

http://www.beamsinvestigations.org/Two%20large%20saucer%20shaped%20obj
ects%20encountered%20by%20family%20in%20car%20Bagshot%20Heath%20Sur
rey%20United%20Kingdom%20September%2015,%201985.htm

for the report of two large saucer-shaped objects that were encountered by a family in a car in Bagshot Heath, Surrey.

Then there was Guildford: Yet more UFO's for the area.

15 years-worth of previously unseen UFO files opened-up by the National Archives, revealed a noteworthy sighting report for Guildford.

Two objects measuring 'elbow to finger size' were spotted for a couple of minutes hovering above the railway bridge footpath in Woodbridge Hill, Guildford, July 1994 at 10:20pm.

The unidentifieds, described as having a brown-grey colour, were spotted during a clear night, and reported to police 12 hours later.

Logic dictates that early man is likely to have commemorated UFO events like these by marking the viewing points accordingly with his special edifices.

Then next, as tradition changed through the epochs, 'the church', (unwittingly perhaps) kept such sacredness alive by raising their edifices over Pagan sites, in a way, following in their predecessors' footsteps.

**Now, our hunt switches five miles north of Worthing, West Sussex, on top of the South Downs escarpment.**

Among the 8 assessed geo-lines running through this location, I have selected one which displayed the highest quality of historical constituents.

Advancing east, we can trace our ley to Sullington Hill, its prehistoric Cross Dyke, then onwards to the Frieslands Tumulus site.

Another Cross Dyke comes next, before the alignment connects with Chanctonbury Ring Earthwork, then on to Trueleigh Hill and Edburton Church,

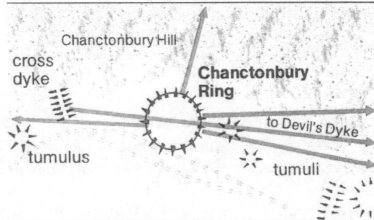

which are also way-markers.

Continuing on route, this 'leyne' passes through The Devils Dyke at Poynings, before hitting an unnamed Tumuli site.

Finally, the line journeys through Lewes Castle, (C11 & C14 fortification remains, but which are recorded as being built on the site of a far earlier 'ritualistic' position) and a nearby Barrow, before passing off the map.

For those who know anything about Pagan folklore, Chanctonbury Ring is certainly a name to conjure with.

Having been initially advised by fellow enthusiasts that at least 30 Ley Lines cut through this site, my partner and I decided to find out more for ourselves by embarking on several intensive missions there.

That figure of 30 was a bit optimistic to say the least.

We couldn't verify anywhere near that number of lines, but of those we did manage to confirm, this as I say, is the best of the bunch.

Situated at a lofty elevation of some 782 feet above sea level, Chanctonbury Hill is certainly not a climb for the feint-hearted; but when one reaches its zenith, a spot perfectly aloof from that social folly called *progress*, can be enjoyed.

At this slightly dizzy height one can absorb some stunning views of the Sussex Weald landscape, which are well worth the climb alone.

Up there, we were met with a grove of spindly beech and sycamore trees, otherwise known colloquially as 'the ring'.

Handbooks generally catalogue this recess as having once contained an Iron Age Hillfort, (from around 600 BC) yet a pamphlet obtained from the Worthing Museum projects a somewhat different picture.

Its writing conjectures whether Chanctonbury Ring 'may also have once been a religious site'.

The same publication furthers matters; 'a temple certainly stood here during the Romano-British period; as the excavated remains of an ornate 'tesserae floor', (made from cubes of coloured stone) and a tiled roof testify'.

Having established this much, some literature of the nearby Steyning museum informs us what this 'temple' was likely to have been used for; it 'was the centre of a cult'.

But expect to see Chanctonbury's finest archaeological artefacts on display, either locally or at Worthing, and one will be sorely disappointed.

The reason for this curio insufficiency? Aha, the small print at the bottom of one of these official brochures spells out exactly what has happened here...

'Chanctonbury is part of a private estate and 'most finds from the site have been retained by the owners.'

'The Goring family acquired this hill in the eighteenth century, and still has proprietorship today'.

There were 3 mysterious deaths that occurred in this vicinity over a 6-year period.

The coroner was forced to return open verdicts in all three cases due to the advanced state of decomposition of the bodies.

The first such case was that of Police Constable Peter Goldsmith in 1972.

Goldsmith, 46, was a former Royal Marine Commando and an experienced rambler who was in excellent physical condition. He was last seen in June that year, walking across the Downs and carrying a large holdall. His body was found six months later hidden in a patch of thick bramble.

In August 1975, pensioner Leon Foster was found in the woods, by a couple searching for a lost horse, three weeks after his wife had reported him missing.

And then the Reverend Harry Neil Snelling – the retired vicar of Clapham Parish – disappeared on All Hallows Eve in 1978 while returning home across the Downs from a dental appointment in Goring; his body was eventually found three years later by a Canadian tourist, who only informed the police of his discovery after he had left the country. Source: northstandchat.com

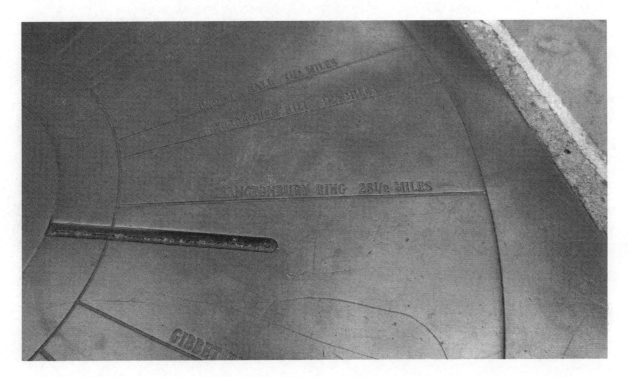

Taken from a modern Trigonometry point at Crooksbury Hill, Farnham, Surrey looking out towards Chanctonbury Hill, Sussex; this is just some 28 miles distant from here… that is, if you travel in a straight line across country!

## People of The Stones

Looking out from the immediate environs of Chanctonbury using binoculars, and our attention was captured by an interesting bell tower pointing out from the backwoods canopy.

It was the church of Saint Andrews, a few miles distant in Steyning.

Next day we paid a visit there in the hope of learning more.

A shrewd move indeed: For nestled away inside the porch of this church were two extremely aged stone monoliths.

Upon closer inspection, we found that the slightly smaller of the duo carried some religious motifs, crudely scratched into its surface; but it quickly became apparent that the roots of the biggest mystery here owed very little to Christianity, for the bulkiest of the two stones carried a finely articulated carving of an extremely esoteric nature.

Over the weeks that followed, we immersed ourselves in studying records for this sleepy village whose title of Steyning, (from the Saxon *Stenningas* 5th, 6th centuries A.D. and *Staeningum* C 880) directly means **'People of the Stones'**, which provided us with the necessary rudimentary facts and figures that were necessary to take matters further.

Apparently, the more impressive stone, (which measures a whopping 5ft 8ins and approximately 1' 5' wide) had first yielded its astonishing secret during renovation work in 1938.

The carving had lain for centuries at the eastern end to Steyning's present church, turned face down, partly sunk into the ground and used as a step!

When lifted in 38', workman noticed a baffling Egyptian Hieroglyph occupying the side that had been buried.

'Carved megalith - taken from a nearby high place'

Close up detail showing cuts either end

Today: View from Steyning church looking through the back of this rural town and up to Chanctonbury

Hill. That clump of trees in the near distance is the 'high place' from where the stone was taken.

Yesteryear - the mystical Chanctonbury Ring

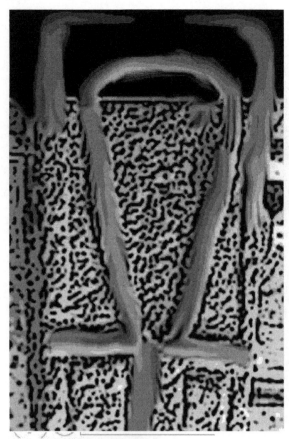

A reconstruction of how our stone may have looked

For illustrative purposes only! This is to prove that 'double ankh's' did indeed exist.
A National Geographic photo showing a rare Kushite gold bracelet from between 785 BC and 350 AD

Archaeological authorities were quickly enlisted to unravel this thriller.

Its geological age and composition were no problem to estimate... verdict – Eocene sandstone; but professedly, its chiselled symbol had the examiners foxed!

When I first set eyes on this artefact it took a few minutes for the potential magnitude to fully sink in.

Then bam!

A wave of excitement suddenly overtook us at the prospect of what we had stumbled upon here.

Grabbing the camera, I said to Hilary, 'quick – I'd better get some pictures of it'... as if the monolith had legs and could suddenly race out of the church at any minute!

After securing many shots with my trusty 35mm SLR, we took time to study the carving in meticulous detail, which left us with no doubt in our minds whatsoever.

A portion had been sheared off either end, (possibly either to transform this into a coffin lid, like its smaller partner, or perhaps having been re-sized for its new use as a church step) it clearly depicted, (or once depicted in full) a double *Crux Ansata* – The Ankh, or Key of Life!

Bearing in mind that phonetically Chanctonbury, has the phonetics of Ch-Ank-Ton-Bury.

The four units of sound are Ch-Ank-Ton-Bury.

A quick check on Google revealed that the 'ank' phonetic in British place names is ultra-rare, in fact we couldn't find any other examples at all; but as mentioned, that wasn't as broad a search as it could have been using physical records, due to reasons of time.

Feasibly, someone can take this further.

A bonus clue to consider, until the late 18th century Chanctonbury was known simply as 'CHANKBURY'. (Chenkburie 1610 and Chankberie in 1587).

The reader will immediately notice from this how the 'K' in 'ank', was subsequently changed to a 'C', thus removing, (to the less probing enquirer) the obvious trace of just how closely this name formerly spoke of 'Ank', with an even stronger suggestion of the 'Ankh' word than it has now since it was altered.

Mere coincidence, or once again, a subtle manipulation of our history? imposed upon us to influence the way that we view our ancient past?

Academics often choose to avoid the real, but largely hidden whys and wherefores of our past, and is it any wonder?

One more point to pick up on is a misnomer concerning the 'Bury' element in place names; because statistics show that more than two thirds of locations with this particular ending, weren't used for burial purposes and neither did they hold fortifications!

Sourcing from a volume published in Antwerp, (1658) which chronicles the exploits of Saint Cuthman, (the man who built the very first church in Steyning – made from wood) and the gradual movement of Christianity westwards through Sussex during the 7th century, I read of a missionary effort known **as 'the conversion of The Manhood Peninsular'**; this is a reference to the southwestern part of Sussex in England, a piece of land almost surrounded by water or projecting out into a body of water… which on some early maps,

does look quite phallic in its shape.

Its author agrees – 'we know the Saxons set up stones in places of worship, often sacred groves, and we remember that the place where Cuthman built his church was formerly wooded'.

'It was a place lying at the base of a lofty hill, then woody, overgrown with brambles and bushes, but now rendered by agriculture fertile and fruitful; enclosed between two streams springing from the hill above'.

The water source here today is still so rich in nutrients, that it's flow, (which seems to trickle either directly under the church or mighty close-by below ground) feeds a lush display of aquatic life to be found not far from St Andrew and St Cuthman.

'We also know that it was the practice of Christian missionaries to build churches on the sites of Pagan worship – so that there could never be any opportunity for a return to Paganism'.

Pope Gregory had given specific instructions on this point in 601 AD.

'So, when Cuthman came, (to Steyning) perhaps he found the stone as the symbol of the local people's identity and their religion.

'Gradually we may imagine him persuading the community that their true identity lay not in relation to a dead stone, but to a living God.

'To persuade the people that the stone had no magic powers and held no threat to a believer in Christ, perhaps Cuthman touched the stone, even sat upon it, and although the priests uttered dire warnings and promised retribution, Cuthman survived.

'Emboldened by his example others followed and like Cuthman survived.'

Across the road from his church... a modern sculpture of a satisfied young Cuthman with one foot firmly on the ankh stone; a celebration of another Christian victory over Paganism.

It is recorded that 'eventually, when his church was built, the stone was dragged from its 'high place' by Cuthman, (which was obviously the summit of a local hill, with the only candidate fitting such a description being Chanctonbury) and dumped'.

Not that I am a particularly religious person, but as a youngster I sat through a few Methodist teachings at my Sunday School classes, and there is one curious biblical quote that has always stuck in my mind; it comes from Proverbs 22- V8 which warns... *'Remove not the ancient landmark that your fathers have set'*; how odd then, for a man of the cloth, (or even any labourer hired by Cuthman for this dirty deed) to disobey the Bible by removing the stone!

But as no artefact fitting this description was known to exist locally, scholars had always satisfied themselves that the village title, (meaning *people of the stones*) referred to the ancient mining of flints; however, the closest location where traces of shafts and galleries, (dating back over 3,000 years ago) have been discovered, is at Cissbury Ring, two and a half miles distant.

'Then in 1938, a stone, used by generations as a step, was unearthed and found to be covered in strange markings', which can now be seen along with a plain pre-Christian standing stone in the church porch.

As a step, it seems to have originally been placed here as part of a symbolic act; perhaps as the worshippers trod on it, they were unknowingly desecrating the old religion as they walked into the church.

Right now, we might ask, what the heck is this Pagan artefact still doing in a house of God anyway? And why was it ever incorporated as part of the building there in the first place?

Was it sited here purely as a trophy symbolising the Christian overpowering of Paganism? or might the early rescue and preservation of such relics by the church really be an indication of something else? That certain clergy of the time secretly harboured some regard for the old wisdom, and perhaps still do?

The use of overturned Pagan stones in churches was once a widespread practise.

A classic example of this came to light in the 1940's, when what looked to be an unusually large, plane flag in the church at Borley, Essex was lifted by workmen;

http://www.real-british-ghosts.com/borley-church.html

after it was raised, they discovered markings on its underside, which confirmed to experts that the slab was in fact a Pagan altar stone.

I finish this section by asking about the most obvious of problems; if this stone does depict the remains of an ankh symbol, (and I am convinced that it does) whether 600 or 1300+ years old, how in heavens name did this piece of Egyptian iconography reach our shores at such an early period?

A couple of years ago – The National Geographic Magazine may have provided a clue that might help solve such out-of-place artefact conundrums, when they exposed a long-running dispute over the authenticity of certain exhibits in the Cairo Museum, Egypt, and the proposal of radio carbon testing on the suspect items.

When this analysis was eventually conducted – the suspicious relics were all verified prehistoric... BUT, more delightfully, (from our standpoint) several lead artefacts positively showed up as being made from metallic elements which could only have originated from one Geological location in the world – Somerset, England!

That parts of our own country were visited by the Phoenicians on many occasions, (such as to Cornwall for *tin, and The Mendips for lead and Sussex for flint is well attested.*More valuable than lead, tin figured somewhat higher on the list of desirable goods in the ancient world, because of its necessity in the making of bronze. As early as 445BC, 'the father of history' Herodotus, spoke of the British Isles as the 'Cassiterides' – the Tin Islands!

When Rome was little more than a hilltop village, Phoenician merchants were already sailing their ships throughout the Mediterranean and beyond in search of commodities to be sold or bartered... all at a time before navigational compasses were invented.

Appraisers may well say, OK, we buy the idea up to a point, but there remains one fundamental flaw in your argument; just how DID anyone manage long-distance navigation to Britain without the aid of a compass?

It is known how natives of the Pacific and other parts of the world possess a gift for instinctive orientation, as they had an inherent knack for navigating by the Sun and stars alone. There is nothing to suggest that the Phoenicians or the Egyptians, lacked this ability.

There are several routes they could have taken to sail to Britain, though the most logical would have been by voyaging across the Mediterranean Sea, through the Gibralter Straits, rounding the Bay of Biscay and across the English Channel.

Aleister Crowley, the infamous Black Magician, who was also a 32nd level Freemason, and his No.1 disciple Victor Neuberg of Steyning, both believed that Chanctonbury Hill was a place of power – and were known to have conducted numerous ritualistic practices there.

Today, local customs for Steyning include The Chanctonbury Ring Morris Men, (one of the oldest Morris dancing sides) whose routine is in the Cotswold style, incorporating a dragon effigy.

They also perform a *Mummers Play on Boxing Day. *What? You've never heard of 'Mumming'?

Sadly, Mummers plays, (once a common sight around the counties of old England) are fast approaching extinction in many districts.

One of the few places where the practice of 'Mumming' can still be witnessed is Church Crookham, Hampshire.

Another point of interest at Church Crookham is 'The Wyvern' public house... believe it or not!

No, not because of its beer, but because upon us entering this watering hole years ago for the first time, we noted, (among a good deal of farming memorabilia on display) a very interesting mounted sign painted with the classic phrase **'anima telluris'** = animated earth... a fine indication of this area's former beliefs.

Back to Sussex again, and one can only take a guess at what happened to those who introduced the Ankh cult to Steyning, and the tribe who fashioned and worshipped the great stone; yet before we depart completely from this area, there's one more point here I need to expand on slightly.

While on the subject of the Mummers, I have learned from author Jaqueline Simpson, who has written a fine book entitled 'Folklore of Sussex' (2002) about a definite connection between Plough Monday and the Mummers custom; Jaqueline obtained this valuable confirmation orally from an elderly informant, that *'when Plough Monday came along all the Tipteers (Mummers) used to dress in white and hang garlands of paper flowers round their necks and bits of ribbends pinned all over, an they dragged a plough round an asked for money at every house. Then they had a feast [a festical]'.*

Within the space of a page or two, you will see how the piquant title of 'Mummers' caused me to delve ever deeper into the whole phenomenon of matriarchal naming, but first, I must give a mention to All Saints Church, Buncton, West Sussex... (located just 3.2 miles from Steyning) whose north impost of the chancel arch sports a carved figure of a pre-Christian fertility deity... often referred to as a Sheela-na-gig.

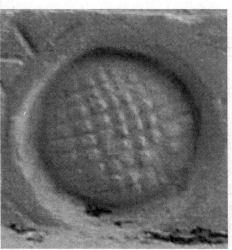

Buncton Chapel's carving; note the secret symbolism located above this figure, (the main detail of which is shown here on the right) ... a code that only those with eyes that truly see would recognise; you can take or leave my theory as to what this represents. I am not attempting to force this on anyone, but merely putting out an idea which deeply resonates within me as the truth; I believe that this circular grid pattern marking is an earth fertility message. One printed account I examined, which was written by Sussex Archaeological Research, suggested about this place that 'the obvious Norman origin of the church doesn't preclude the possibility of a previous building on the site as the name of the place suggests and with the spring in close proximity, there may even have been a Roman temple in the area.'

Yet, what you have here is not entirely how this carving used to be; because in December 2004, some nutjob entered the church and destroyed the carving with a chisel, obliterating its vagina... a real Pagan whodunnit!

All Saints Church is an Anglican church in the hamlet of Buncton in the district of Horsham, (formerly Wiston)

Sheela-Na-Gig on Church of St Mary and St David in Kilpeck

Although we don't have a photo to prove that originally the Buncton female figure WAS exhibiting her genitalia as mentioned, I am absolutely convinced that is the case; because as the above image from a church in Kilpeck, Herefordshire clearly shows, that IS the purpose of the Sheela-na-gig; this Christian/Pagan flirtation represents the goddess of fertility in British-Celtic mythology promoting fertility and the living earth concept.

 There are some other survivors of such church carvings, (like this 14th century example from St Laurence's in Church Stretton Shropshire) but they are uncommon, with many suspected to have been allowed to erode away by environmental factors, and others having met the same fate as our Buncton friend, mostly at the hands of church Reformists.

Apart from their usual meanings, I found the words 'Mummy' and 'Mum' had at least two other antiquated, horticultural/agricultural links.

In an academic volume by Samuel Johnson, LL. D printed in 1863, 'Mummy' is listed as 'a sort of wax used in the planting and grafting of trees'.

I also came across 'Mummy' catalogued in far more obscure works as...'a substance sold by the Apothecary to be used medicinally'.

In addition, the Samuel Johnson publication cites 'Mum' as 'an ale brewed with wheat'.

Spurred on by these finds, I conducted further studies involving relative linguistics.

A broader range of words containing the universalist 'Ma' epithet, (as touched on earlier) began to take on a new complexion.

Terms such as:

<u>Ma</u>p> a diagrammatic representation of the earth's surface.

<u>Ma</u>trix, <u>Ma</u>gnetism and <u>Ma</u>thematics.

Also staying within the bounds of reason, we can now consider the titles of all these Mother Earth Rocks and Ores:

<u>Ma</u>gnesia > oxide of Magnesium.

<u>Ma</u>gma> volcanic mixture of minerals in a thin, pasty state.

<u>Ma</u>lachite> a green coloured stone, native carbonate of copper.

<u>Ma</u>lacolite> a variety of augite.

<u>Ma</u>lmrock> a calcareous sandstone.

<u>Ma</u>mmaliferous> a geological term meaning rock-bearing mamiferous remains.

<u>Ma</u>nganite> an ore of manganese.

<u>Ma</u>rble> a veined calcareous stone.

<u>Ma</u>rcasite> iron pyrites.

<u>Ma</u>rgode> a hard, bluish-grey stone.

And what of words like:

<u>Ma</u>melon> a rounded mound (Fr. from L. mamma – 'the breast').

<u>Ma</u>mmee> an apple, the produce of a fruit tree of tropical America.

<u>Mandala> in Hindu and Buddhist art, a Mandala is any of various, (usually circular) designs symbolising the universe.</u>

Manhood> virility.

Manna> from the Old Testament; 'the miraculous food which sustained the Israelites in the wilderness.

Marabuts> A priestly caste of North Africa.

Market and Market Garden> Orig: medieval *Greek* and *Roman* 'Macellum> a covered market where fish, fruit and vegetables (e.g. Mackerel, Marrow, Mango, Mandrake, Marjoram and Maize etc) might be offered for sale.

*Maya> an American Indian people of the Yucatan, Belize and N. Guatemala who once worshipped Chalchihuitlicue - the goddess of the Green Gown. **Another cultural shocker: In Mayan, the word 'chuch' or 'church' literally means 'earth'.**

Then there are… Brahma, ('The World Soul' of Hindu culture) Mammal, Mandarin, Marine, Marsh, Muhammad; we have **The Maha Kumbh Mela**, (*the annual Hindu celebration of ritualistic bathing in the 'Holy Mother' Ganges, Northern India) **The Masai Mara tribe (of Africa)** Marsupial, Martyr, Masculine… all self-explanatory bearers of the 'Ma' syllable; same goes for Ramadan. *Also, to be taken into consideration are these other Indian Holy Days, that are all held during important Moon cycles:

The Makar Sankranti  - January 14; The Mahvir Jayanti – April 6; The Budh Poornima – May 7th and The Janmashtmi – August 12th.

Many religious festivals are determined by an actual sighting of the appropriate New Moon and therefore dates given are only an approximation.

Extract from the Brahman 'Upanishad'; 1V. 8 – 1V.14

'Know that all of nature is but a magic theatre, that the Great Mother is the master magician… and that the whole world is peopled by her many parts.'

So, it goes on and on and on, almost *ad nauseum* - just too many to mention.

I've left plenty more for the reader to find.

With most of this book now in place, the view is one of an ancient, sophisticated knowledge about our earth - and human interaction with a non-human super intelligence.

But despite what we and others may say, many will continue to embrace without question, exactly what mainstream religion tells them, blindly accepting everything as completely normal; but I suppose there's nothing wrong with that... it's all good stuff, any form of worship is preferable to a totally faithless society; the only thing I do object to, is how, those who are blinkered to the truth often feel obliged to attack anything labelled 'new age' or 'occult'.

**Natural Law**

To the closed mind, absolutely no credence can be given to the idea that the established church is one giant heirloom containing an encoded Pagan wisdom.

For minds vanquished by the standard saviour-god religions, what I have written will not constitute one single shred of evidence in favour of the secret, lost knowledge proposal.

Yet, even taking away the whole Pagan versus theological argument, most of us are still shown to be the victims of foul play.

Just consider the seemingly abstract concept of Time Travel if you will.

One could be pardoned for having visions of *Star Trek* or *Doctor Who* at the very mention of these words; but contrary to what is generally assumed, this topic should not be dismissed as fiction; not when you think, that whenever we survey the night sky, we are in effect looking back in time.

Starlight is a **Living Energy**, which has taken thousands, millions or even billions of years to reach earth.

This thing we call 'time', (as a coordinate) doesn't flow in only one direction either.

To an extent, time is illusory, being purely dependent on the observers' frame of reference between two separate events.

Another little-publicised antithesis to popular belief is the area space all around us... that apparent void surrounding everything.

Celebrated mathematician, Albert Einstein, addressed this very problem when campaigning his 'Multiverse' theorem.

He said, 'the whole of our reality is manifested by the geometrics of space and time.'

'Empty space has no practical meaning; space cannot exist separately from what fills space, and the geometry of space is determined by the matter it contains'.

'There is no such thing as nothing'.

Amongst his voluminous writing and lectures, Einstein aired his suspicions that space is 'multiversal'.

For decades, physicists have presumed that space-time has just four special dimensions in total – 3 of space and 1 of time; but some professors have proposed that there may be additional dimensions that we don't sense in our everyday lives.

This is the way I see it: Earth is probably best described as being rather like a multi-dimensional 'onion', and space could contain a myriad of differing atomic and molecular layers or frequencies; with us, (physical life) on the outer skin, every layer of the onion would represent an overlapping, (perhaps intertwining) Universe; each coexisting with its neighbour, but always invisible to one-another because of the differing molecular frequencies involved.

Who can say for sure?

Perhaps the European Organization for Nuclear Research (CERN) can.

These are the guys who built The Large Hadron Collider (LHC).

It was constructed between 1998 and 2008 in collaboration with over 10,000 scientists and hundreds of universities and laboratories, as well as more than 100 countries. It lies in a tunnel 27 kilometres in circumference and as deep as 175 metres (574 ft) beneath the France/Switzerland border near Geneva.

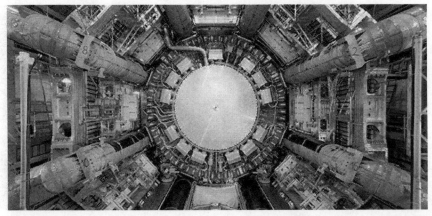

Very much on CERN's agenda is the search for multidimensional objects; but does the reader think that physicists will keep the public informed if they ever do discover anything so significant?

In 2012 they did announce a discovery... of a new particle, which was later confirmed to be the Higgs boson, an elementary particle in the Standard Model of particle physics.

Smithsonian.com reported the publication of an exciting new book by Harvard University theorist Lisa Randall, entitled *Knocking on Heaven's Door - How Physics and Scientific Thinking Illuminate the Universe and the Modern World.*

Her work explores how physics may 'transform our understanding of the fundamental nature of the world. **She thinks an extra dimension may exist close to our familiar reality, hidden except for a bizarre sapping of the strength of gravity as we see it.** She also ponders the makeup of dark matter, unseen particles that have shaped the growth of the entire cosmos.

These ideas, once the sole province of fiction writers, face real tests in a new generation of experiments. Sensitive detectors now sniff for dark matter, while the most complex scientific machine ever created, the Large Hadron Collider

(LHC) beneath the border of Switzerland and France, smashes subatomic particles into one another at almost the speed of light.

Lisa was asked: *If physicists do find solid evidence of extra dimensions, how would that affect our view of the universe and our place in it?*

She answered: 'You can have very exotic underlying phenomena; it means that at some deep level, there's a much richer universe out there. It's just a wonderful thing to know what our universe is made of.' End quote.

I do have a habit of repeating myself, (sorry about that) but for me, the concept of space-time dimensions isn't that far removed from the famous Biblical narrative of God describing earth as his 'house of many mansions'. [dimensions?]

Add to this, another cat let out of the scientific bag not so long ago, when a prominent astrophysicist defied all expectations by commenting; 'we are making measurements that indicate the universe is filled with some kind of energy density; we don't understand this energy at all; its unlike anything else in physical theory'.

I also noticed that The Independent newspaper website was reporting on a then 'brand-new' experiment, (this time based in the U.S.) at seeing into hidden worlds. 'Could 2019 be the year humans open the first portal to a shadowy dimension which mirrors our own world?

Scientists in Oak Ridge National Laboratory in eastern Tennessee hope so, and have completed building equipment they are to test this summer which may allow us the first glimpse of a parallel universe which could be identical in many ways to our own, with mirror particles, mirror planets and possibly even mirror life.

That is according to Leah Broussard, the physicist behind this project, who described the attempt to reveal a hidden shadow world as "pretty wacky" in an interview with NBC last week.

The discovery of a concealed mirror world may sound like science fiction from the Stranger Things series, but it has been repeatedly suggested by physicists as a tempting means of explaining anomalous results. However, as yet, hard evidence that such a realm exists has refused to manifest itself.

One set of anomalous results, and the ones which inspired the research, date back to the 1990s, when particle physicists were measuring the time it took for neutron particles to break down into protons once they were removed from an atom's nucleus.

Two separate experiments saw the neutrons broke down at differing rates, instead of decaying and becoming protons at the same rate, as was expected.

In one, the free neutrons were captured by magnetic fields and herded into laboratory bottle traps, and in the other they were detected by the subsequent appearance of proton particles from a nuclear reactor stream.

Those particles fired out in the stream from the nuclear reactor lived on average for 14 minutes and 48 seconds – nine seconds longer than those from the bottle traps.

It may sound like a small difference, but it has troubled scientists.

But the existence of a mirror world offers a credible explanation: That there are two separate neutron lifetimes, and it could be that around 1 per cent of neutrons are crossing the divide between our reality and the mirror world before crossing back and then emitting a detectable proton.

The new experiment will fire a beam of neutrons at an impenetrable wall. On the other side of the wall, a neutron detector will be set up, which normally would expect to detect nothing.

But if the detector does register the presence of neutrons, the theory is that they may have gone through the wall by "oscillating" into the mirror world – becoming mirror neutrons then reappearing in this universe, and more specifically the lab in Tennessee.

"Only the ones that can oscillate and then come back into our universe can be detected," Ms Broussard told the New Scientist in June.

Furthermore, the team will set up magnetic fields on either side of the wall, which they can alter in strength. It is hoped certain strengths may assist the oscillation of the particles.

Despite this tidy theory, the team is playing down the chances of revealing reality's shadowy twin.

"I fully expect to measure zero," Ms Broussard said of the initial tests.

But if they do detect a neutron on the far side of the wall, it could have profound implications.

"If you discover something new like that, the game totally changes," Ms Broussard told NBC.

The existence of a mirror world could also explain our universe's lack of the isotope Lithium 7, which physicists believe doesn't match the quantities The Big Bang would have created.

The detection of high-energy cosmic rays which come from beyond our galaxy could also be explained by the existence of the mirror world.

They are too powerful to have travelled only through the observed universe, but if they had oscillated into the mirror realm and then back out again, it could explain why that is the case.'

## Metempsychosis

The grapevine rumours are strong, that behind closed doors those who *are in the know* already speak in terms of at least 16 dimensions… parallel universes or alternate realities that exist parallel to our own.

Another potential clue for us is something known as the **Morphogenetic Field**.

This term was first applied in the late 1920's and is now frequently used by developmental biologists practically everywhere.

**The 'field' refers to a strong likelihood that an inherited recall, (or memory 'resonance') resides in everything.**

The Morphogenetic Field can be envisioned as a hyperspatial information reservoir that brims and spills over into a much larger region of influence when critical mass is reached – a point referred to as Morphic Resonance.

As well as all things animate, it is speculated that shape and form carry their very own special vibratory fields also.

Is this 'field' an actual demonstration of 'Metempsychosis' (referring to a 'continued existence after death in a different manner or form') as Pythagoras, (often referred to as the first pure mathematician c. 570 – c. 495 BC) is said to have called it?

Imagine the potential ramifications if this 'field' was widely proven to exist.

**The Day the Sun Went Out**

During the initial stages of my research, I had often wondered why the worship of earth deities had been revived worldwide in such a prolific way around the 6$^{th}$ century AD.

Just what was it about this era I mused, that could have caused such a resurgence of interest in Paganism? especially when one considers the onslaught of Christianity taking place at that time.

As it happens, the outcome of a mammoth survey conducted by scientific teams throughout the world, might have answered my question with a vengeance.

*Channel 4 Television's* epic documentary series *Secrets of the Dead* came up trumps, when scholar David Keys showed the 6$^{th}$ century to be a period when a catastrophic climatic hiccup occurred.

Using exhaustive dendrological examinations, (the study of tree rings) and ice sample analysis, Keys and his fellow researchers found evidence of a massive volcanic discharge for the year 535 AD.

The likeliest candidate was Krakatoa, Indonesia, (located in the Sundra Strait between Java and Sumatra) a geologically active island which has blown its top on numerous occasions.

But this was the mother of ALL discharges, calculated to have been the equivalent of **two billion Hiroshima bombs** being detonated simultaneously!

Atmospheric carbon detected for that year, told of a virtual nuclear-winter scenario.

According to estimations, the sun was largely obscured for upwards of five years by trillions of tons of ash particles discharged high into the air.

The calamity caused, is likely to have affected many countries worldwide... Britain included, but to a lesser extent than some other parts.

Much of earth's ecosystem would have suffered considerably, heralding famines and warring.

Following these stimulating findings, the usual dictionary designation for 'the Dark Ages' as meaning 'an unenlightened period in our past'…

[but then think of **un-en-lightened** phonetically, as in **'no light'**, and maybe the answer has been staring us in the face for donkey's years],

…now took on a whole new complexion.

Can anyone seriously believe that once the gloom had lifted from such a catastrophe – nature would be taken for granted?

On the contrary, Gods could be capable of exceptional cruelty and run out of patience when displeased with man; that was part-and-parcel of the Pagan rationale.

It was not difficult therefore to envisage a concerted attempt at appeasement of Gaia's wrath, following the day when the sun went out.

Common sense decrees how the remainder of humankind, having emerged from the darkness, would have awarded the land a reverence beyond anything now conceivable.

Gaia and Green Man must have come into their own as the soul, creatrix and overseer of nature.

The struggle faced by Christianity during those times in its attempts at eradicating customary religions, must have been Herculean.

But their promotional tactics and sheer persistence eventually prevailed.

By the 9th century, churches had sprung up all over the land, with many blatantly raised on Pagan sites.

The spectacle of these impressive new constructions lured families in from surrounding areas.

Small communities soon swelled into townships; and in lots of instances, much that was previously held sacred, became neglected.

Redundant Pagan temples were ruthlessly cannibalised for their stone; groves cut down for fuel, and water sources, once clear and sparkling, virtually turned into open sewers.

Inevitably, this overcrowding, poor sanitation, and lack of respect for nature led to disease and increased consumption of natural resources.

Against all the odds, small pockets of opposition to the 'new way' stubbornly remained, particularly in remote regions.

And as time wore on, the churches' efforts to win these stragglers over became a protracted battle...

**A Few Related Curios**

Standing smack-bang on a huge ley line, Guildford Cathedral, Stag Hill, was used as a scene backdrop for the creepy 1976 movie *The Omen*; yet, even away from such works of fiction, this location is no stranger to genuine supernatural happenings.

2 photographs taken in April 2012, that appeared to show a spooky shape on The Mount in Guildford, have caused a stir among investigators of The Paranormal.

Amateur photographer, Mark Baker, 37, took the pictures when trying out a new camera timer, and when he downloaded them to his PC, they appeared to show a ghostly white form.

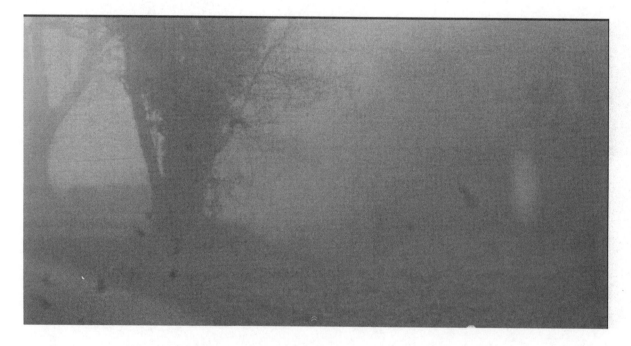

'It was not until I got home and was downloading, I noticed it,' he said; and Mark went on to stress that he had not digitally altered the images in any way.

Pub. 27 May 1785 by S.Hooper.    Mother Ludlam's Hole, Surry.    Sparrow Sc.

## Mother Ludlum's 'Other Hole' is in Guildford

Records show that there is a small, narrow opening in Guildford, (a 'hole' if you like) leading to a natural subterranean rock passage.

Although barely big enough for an adult to squeeze through, this eventually leads to another hole, popularly known as Mother Ludlum's 'Hole', an artificially widened outflow cave with a spring stream running through and from it.

The main entrance of the cave is located in a sandstone cliff at Moor Park near Farnham, Surrey, but is now closed-off to the public due to safety concerns following a partial collapse of its roof.

Folklore suggests that in the 13th century the 'Ludewell', (other spellings through history include 'Ludwell' and 'Luddwell') was once home to a White Witch known as 'Mother' who supplied the nearby *Waverley Abbey, (now a ruin after being dismantled in 1536 under the Dissolution of Monasteries act) with fresh water and cooking utensils in return for food. *It is worth a quick mention that Waverley Abbey is where both my partner and I had rather a good UFO sighting while skywatching there back in 2010; the grounds are reputed to be haunted also.

Origins of the name 'Ludwell' or 'Luddwell. A modern ethnographer would identify 'Lud' as a Celtic god: A temple dedicated to Llud once stood at the site of St. Paul's Cathedral in London near Ludgate, which was named after him.

He replaced the Goddess Tamesis as God of the River Thames.

<u>Llud was also known as the Celtic god of healing.</u>

Of course, that quaint little story of 'Mother's' arrangement with the monks may be just folklore; and looking at the legend another way, (from a Pagan, living earth belief angle) the 'Mother' reference might just as easily be considered as alluding to the 'Earth Mother', (rock womb of) and the 'Hole', a symbolic reference to the opening where the water emerges from 'her' cavernous vagina... now there's a thought!

Mother Ludlum's Cave.

Curiously, on the bank above Mother Ludlam's Cave there once existed another, much smaller cave.

This was allegedly the shelter of a man named 'Foote', who is supposed to have excavated the hollow; locals referred to it as 'Father Foote's Cave'.

Here is yet another connection to the high strangeness of this place.

Above is a genuine picture of the 'spirit' extra of a 'caver' or possibly a miner - taken in the 1960's, during an exploration of Mother Ludlum's Hole, near Farnham, Surrey, UK.

The idea was for the men to crawl through a tight passage at the back of this cave and come out at the Guildford opening.

The person sitting front-right was someone I knew named George, and one day, while he was reminiscing to me about his potholing adventures, he gave me this unusual old photograph to keep; George explained to me that there were only four members in his caving expedition (three of whom are in this picture and one is taking the photo) he had no idea how the fifth man, (highlighted by a circle back-left) got into the shot, as there was absolutely no one else around at the time this was taken.

George said that when he picked his photographs up after processing - he had 'quite a shock' to see this mystery figure 'posing for the camera as bold as brass'; and apparently 'he' was in none of the other shots taken in the cave entrance either.

Note also how the mystery person is not wearing a protective hat; cavers always wear a hard hat with chin strap to protect the head from jagged rocks and possible falling debris.

In my opinion it is unfeasible for this to be a double exposure, as the unknown person is so tightly positioned next to one of the cavers... and like George said, it's as if he's 'posing for the camera'... and no one else saw him.

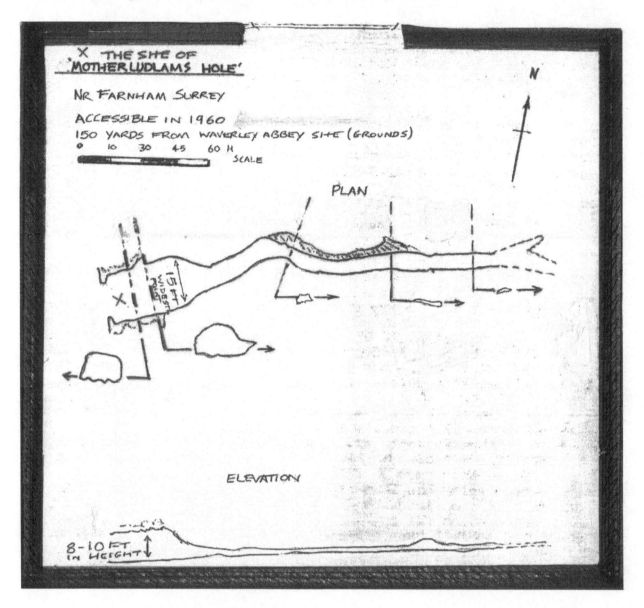

A map that George drew for me to explain how he crawled through from the cave near Farnham to Guildford

Of course, we tend to automatically label these photographic apparitions as 'ghosts' or 'spirits', but it is perhaps worth considering that some so-called 'ghosts' might be the result of another kind of little understood phenomena... residual human memories.

These can somehow become imprinted, (recorded) into the area space of our environment; like a loop of film that is replayed when certain, (psychic?) criteria are fulfilled, as with this grouping of like minds? Yet, such a hypothesis surely only works when a 'ghost' is seen in real time, by the naked eye - or captured on video.

If what we are discussing here is simply some kind of dumb 'ether recording', (for want of a better term) how could this figure have presented itself on a still photograph at all? and so carefully positioned as well... implying that the figure had sentience?

I have carefully kept this photo that George presented to me about 20 years ago, on file, along with his account, but hadn't given it much thought since to be honest; but I find it quite a neat piece of synchronicity how his strange picture only <u>now</u> fully comes into its own, tallying perfectly with the recent research that I have conducted for this book concerning Mother Ludlum's cave.

Bits and pieces of evidence turn up in the most unexpected places sometimes; for instance, we discovered that Saint Mary The Virgin Church, Frensham, Surrey houses Mother Ludlum's cauldron, after the witch is alleged to have placed it there 'where it would be safe from the Devil'; fair enough... but why have they now positioned such an obviously Pagan artefact, practically right next to their altar!

Mother's Cauldron - curiously positioned/displayed in Frensham Church, within a few feet from the altar!

## Heresy or Total Logic?

Some fundamental questions about our past have now been addressed, and it is trusted that readers will pursue and find even more answers for themselves.

Smashed and deeply buried over time, the beauty of the truth is that it never completely disappears.

Admittedly, certain bits and pieces of evidence will always struggle to be rediscovered, but the collection of fragments ploughed back up through Ley Lines & Earth Energies - The Rediscovery of a Lost Wisdom, should have helped to provide a fascinating insight into our original belief system.

What we have learned from this entire investigation, is that those who went before us, many, many, moons ago, may well have instinctively known about the existence of differing vibrations or frequencies, despite having no Quantum Physics references by which to evaluate them.

All of the wisest material that I have been able to obtain translates thus; that these people, the shaman of their day, somehow understood that the apparently empty space of nothing actually contains a great deal; conceivably, a godlike planetary intelligence, and certainly associated energy fields that are usually inaccessible to our limited senses of today; domains accessed by extrasensory means, that are far greater and more natural than the synthetic reality that we have built for ourselves presently.

Such appreciation and sensitivity to these singular beliefs have been taught-out... hereditarily bred-out from us over countless generations; teacher after teacher filling our heads with limited, mechanistic ideas.

For most, our '**Internal Alchemy**', (psychic, 'sixth-sense' development, meditative/altered states of awareness) has deserted us; which in turn means that our appreciation of '**Earth Alchemy**', (together with the hermeticism which once enabled our finest occult scholars and their students to enjoy the fruits of possible Paranormal learnings) barely survives.

My advice to those who want to investigate further, the many mysteries that I have been discussing in this book, is as follows:

Don't be afraid to embrace the past as you search for any surviving intelligence about obscure Pagan traditions. Test everything: retain what is good.

Never rely on guidebook-type spiel.

Hold little faith if any, in 'the official line'; our secret overseers believe that an ignorant populace is a **controllable** populace.

Unless they are like-minded people on the same wavelength as you, never discuss your findings with friends, relatives or neighbours; there will be no point; the average person's appreciation will be limited; try talking about the sacrosanct in these uncertain times and you'll soon become a Billy no-mates!

I just wish more people could learn about what I have written here, because despite all of our clever and entertaining technology, today's society is far less morally, spiritually and  mentally satisfied than our Pagan antecedents ever were; in fact, much of mankind has become so self-indulgent that we are having an enormous impact on our planet; humanity has now become like a virus eating away at the earth... and our ever-increasing cycle of 'me', 'me', 'me' is no longer sustainable; earth's resources are fast becoming depleted through our cold, selfishness and over consumption.

The following quote is from a book entitled 'Are You Living or Just Existing?',

https://www.amazon.co.uk/dp/1912400065/ref=as_li_qf_asin_il_tl?ie=UTF8&link Code=gs2&linkId=805605467bf5bee7f473cc8425b323bd&creativeASIN=1912400 065&tag=dreamcatche04-21&creative=9325

which sums things up perfectly.

'Today's children are growing up more connected digitally than ever before; yet [they] have never been more disconnected from their natural surroundings. Most children know how to download apps long before they can name the types of birds and wildlife found in their very own gardens'... 'our love of technology transcends our love of what is real and organic which leads me to wonder where this will all end?'.

For me, the moral of what we are presently seeing in life suggests two things; less is more and abandon superstition at your peril!

It cannot be denied, that currently we are living in ultra-dangerous times on many levels, and I suggest the only way forward, (for some at least) is to take a step back and rediscover the knowledge of our forebears.

I hope the reader agrees, that the radical ideas, clues, and possibilities presented here have offered up some rare insights into the special relationship that can exist between ourselves, the electromagnetic dimensions and entities which surround us, and the Macrocosm.

Now, YOU may believe… the question is, now, WHO is going to believe you?

Thanks for reading.

Some supporting images and quotations herein come under 'educational use', Fair Use Interpretation of Copyright Laws; others are used by permission.

If any reader has relevant information that they would like to share, or questions to ask about this book, then please feel free to email me on…

beamsinvestigations@sky.com

I really do think that some things are preordained and meant to be.

Much appreciated.

# Other Sources and Recommended Reading

Aside from details already featured within text and those obtained courtesy of archives, personal contacts and in-field investigation – the sources listed below were also consulted in the writing of *TGH*. These may prove useful to the student who wishes to pursue matters further.

Subject: Public Deceived – The Conspiracy
Title: The Committee of 300
Author: Dr John Coleman
Publisher: WIR - Division of Joseph Holding Corp.

Subject: Truth Suppression
Title: The Biggest Secret
Author: David Icke
Publisher: Bridge of Love Publications

Subject: U.S Academy of Science Report.
Human Demands Exceeding Earth's Supply.
BBC World, June 24, 2002.

Subject: The Green Man
Title: A little book of The Green Man
Author: Mike Harding
Publisher: Aurum Press.

Subject: John Barleycorn and The Green Man
Title: The Avebury Circle
Author: Michael Dames
Publisher: Thames and Hudson

Subject: Earth Energies
Title: Ancient Energies of the Earth
Author: David Cowan and Ann A. Silk.
Publisher: (?)

Subject: Water Memory:
Title: Science Frontiers #77
Author: William. R. Corliss.
Associated information can be
obtained by e-mailing **info@alivewater.net**

Subject: Underground Streams.
Title: The Immense Journey
Author: Loren Eiseley
Publisher: Vintage Books. 1959.

Subject: Landscape Alignments
Title: Eleusis Alesia
Author: Xavier Guichard
Publisher: F. Paillart, Abbeville, 1936.

Subject: Ley Lines
Title: Earth Magic
Author: Francis Hitching
Publisher: Pan Books. 1976.

Subject: Anglo-Saxon Earth Rites
Title: Atlantis of the North
Author: Jurgen Spanuth
Publishers: Sidgwick and Jackson. 1979.

Subject: Traces of Gaia Worship
Title: Secret Places of the Goddess
Author: Philip Heselton
Publisher: Capall Bann. 1995

Subject: The Secrets Folklore and Custom
Title: The Lost Language of Symbolism
Author: Harold Bayley
Publisher: Chapman and Hall.

Subject: Lost Landscape Wisdom.
Title: Archaic England
Author: Harold Bayley
Publisher: Chapman and Hall. 1919

**Further reading – also worth tracking down through specialist outlets, book-finding services and museums.**

Palaeomagnetism and its Application to Geological and Geophysical Problems by E. Irving:
Publisher John Wiley and Sons Inc. 1964

Neolithic Engineering by R.J.C. Atkinson. pp.292-9: Publisher Macmillan: 1906. (may be examined in
British Museum Reading Rooms).

Field Archaeology in Britain, (which also covers alignments and connections), by John Coles:
Publisher Methuen. 1972

The Devil and All His Works by Dennis Wheatley: Hutchinson Publishing Co: 1971

Ley Lines by Danny Sullivan: Publisher, Piatkus. 1999.

# Other Sources and Recommended Reading

Aside from details already featured within text and information obtained courtesy of archives, personal contacts and in-field investigation – the sources listed below were also consulted in the writing of *TGH*: These may prove useful to the student who wishes to pursue matters further.

Subject: Druidical Knowledge
Title: The Mysteries of Britain: Secret Rites and Traditions of Ancient Britain
Author: Lewis Spence
Publisher: Senate. Studio Editions.

Subject: Earth Rites
Title: *Funebria Florae* pp 6 & 16
Author: Thomas Hall . . . 1661.

Subject: The Bible Conspiracy
Title: Scroll #123
Author: Dr M. Z. York
Author: HTM c/o P.O. Box 4490, Eatonton, G.A. 31024. U.S.

Subject: Word Etymology
Title: New Websters Dictionary of the English Language
Publisher: Belair Publishing.

Subject: Song of the Seasons (Verse)
Title: Lid off the Cauldron
Author: Patricia Crowther
Publisher: Frederick Muller Ltd, London, 1981.

Subject: The Gregorian Calendar and Other Secrets of the Vatican
Title: Our Ancestors Came From Outer Space – a NASA expert confirms
Author: Maurice Chatelain
Publisher: Pan Books, 1980.

Subject: Morris/Maypole/Mumming and other Lost Knowledge
Title: The Lost Language of Symbolism
Author: Harold Bayley.
Publishers: Chapman and Hall, 1935, (also seek and read 'Archaic England' by same author and publisher.)

Subject: English Wayfaring Life in the Middle Ages
Author: J.J Jusserand, (French Ambassador at Washington).
Publisher: T .Fisher Unwin, (19th century).

Subject: Cult of the Earth Mother
Title: Aztecs of Mexico
Author: G.C. Vaillent
Publisher: Pelican Books. 1950.
Subject: Joanna Southcott and The Panacea Society
Title: Satan's Mistress
Author: Val Lewis
Publisher: Nauticalia Ltd.

**Further reading – also worth tracking down through specialist outlets, book-finding services and museums.**

The White Goddess by Robert Graves: Publisher, Faber and Faber, London. 1961.

The Pattern of the Past by Guy Underwood: Publisher, Abacus. 1972

Pendulum Dowsing by Francis Hitching: Publisher, 1978.
(In the United States, this same book is called *Dowsing: The Psi Connection*: Publisher Anchor/Doubleday).

# Other Sources and Recommended Reading

Aside from details featured within text and information obtained courtesy of archives, personal contacts and in-field investigation – the sources listed below were also consulted in the writing of *TGH*. These may prove useful to the student who wishes to pursue matters further.

Subject: Fulcanelli
Title: Fulcanelli: Master Alchemist
Author: Mary Sworder
Publisher: Neville Spearman. 1980

Subject: Fulcanelli
Title: The Fulcanelli Phenomenon
Author: Kenneth Rayner Johnson
Publisher: Neville Spearman. 1980.

Subject: Black Virgins
Title Mysteries
Author: Colin Wilson
Publisher: Hodder and Stoughton. 1978.
Subject: Black Virgins

Subject: Fulcanelli
Title: The Underground Stream and Fulcanelli's Message.
Author: Jay Weidner and Vincent Bridges
**www.sangraal.com**

Subject: The Sacred Geometry of Chartres
Title: The Atlas of Mysterious Places
Publisher: Guild Publishing, London. 1987.

Subject: Harmonic Field Theory
Title: The Pulse of the Universe, Harmonic 288
Author: Bruce Cathie
Publisher: Sphere. 1981.

**Further reading – also worth tracking down through specialist outlets, book-finding services and museums.**

Energy & The Earth Machine by Donald E. Carr: Publisher Abacus . 1978.

The Mystic Spiral by Jill Purce: Publisher Thames and Hudson. 1974.

# Other Sources and Recommended Reading

Aside from details already featured within text and those obtained courtesy of museum archives, personal contacts and in-field investigation – the sources listed below were also consulted in the writing of *TGH*: These may prove useful to the student who wishes to pursue matters further.

Subject: Subject: Egyptian Ritual
Title: Prophecy Fulfilled
Author: HTM
Publisher: HTM - P.O. Box 4490, Eatonton,
GA. 31024.

Subject: Isis and Osiris
Title: The Green Man
Author: Ronald Millar
Publisher: S.B. Publications, 1998.

Subject: Genesis
Title: The Bible Code
Author: M. Drosnin
Publisher: Weidenfeld Nicholson.

Subject: Earth Forces
Title: Mysteries
Author: Colin Wison
Publisher: Hodder and Stoughton, 1978.

Subject: Ground Radio
*J Noll in Patent 1,365,579 "Radio Apparatus".
*"Underground Loop Antenna" 1,373,612 by Earl C.Hanson.
*www://borderlands.com

Subject: World Lines
Title: The Paranormal, Beyond Sensory Science
Author: Dr Percy Seymour
Publisher: Arkana Books

Subject: Place Names
Title: The Popular Dictionary of English Place Names
Author: A. D. Mills
Publisher: Paragon and Oxford University Press.

**Further reading – also worth tracking down through specialist outlets, book-finding services and museums.**

The Egyptians by
Cyril Aldred, (updated by Alan Dodson),
Published by Thames and Hudson, 1998.

The Concise Oxford Dictionary of English Place Names, 4th edition: Oxford University Press: 1960.

# Other Sources and Recommended Reading

Aside from details already featured within text and those obtained courtesy of museum archives, personal contacts and in-field investigation – the sources listed below were also consulted in the writing of *TGH*: These may prove useful to the student who wishes to pursue matters further.

Subject: Avebury.
Title: The Avebury Circle
Author: Michael Dames
Publisher: Thames and Hudson

Subject: Ley Lines
Title: The Old Straight Track
Author: Alfred Watkins.
Publisher: Methuen & Co (1925), re-issued by Garnstone Press, 1970.

Subject: Place Names
Title: The Popular Dictionary of English Place Names
Author: A. D. Mills
Publisher: Paragon and Oxford University Press.

Subject: Stone Circles in China
p.p.47: UFO Magazine; Feb 2002.

Subject: Chanctonbury and Steyning
Title: The Green Man
Author: Ronald Millar
Publisher: S. B. Publications. 1998.

Subject: Glastonbury
Title: Glastonbury Tales
Author: John A. Greed
Publisher: St Trillo Publications, 1975.

Subject: Gog and Magog
Title: Gogmagog: The Buried Gods
Author: T.C. Lethbridge
Publisher: Routledge and Kegan Paul Ltd. London, 1957.

Subject: William of Malmesbury and Glastonbury.
Title: Sacred England
Author: John Michell
Publisher: Gothic Image.

**Further reading – also worth tracking down through specialist outlets, book-finding services and museums.**

A Guide For Life: Celtic Mysticism by Anthony Duncan, Published by Anness Publishing: 2000.

The Illuminati Formula to Create an Undetectable, Total, Mind-Controlled Slave. Available from Springmeier, SE Clackamas Road, Clackamas, Oregon, 97015: Printed in 1996.

Printed in Great Britain
by Amazon

19351879R00106